MW00412740

CULTURE

Devdutt Pattanaik writes, illustrates and lectures on the relevance of mythology in modern times. He has, since 1996, written over thirty books and 700 columns on how stories, symbols and rituals construct the subjective truth (myths) of ancient and modern cultures around the world. His books include *7 Secrets of Hindu Calendar Art* (Westland), *Myth=Mithya: A Handbook of Hindu Mythology* (Penguin), *Jaya: An Illustrated Retelling of the Mahabharata* (Penguin), *Sita: An Illustrated Retelling of the Ramayana* (Penguin), *Olympus: An Indian Retelling of the Greek Myths* (Penguin), *Business Sutra: A Very Indian Approach to Management* (Aleph), *My Gita* (Rupa) and *Devlok with Devdutt Pattanaik* (Penguin). To know more, visit devdutt.com.

CULTURE

50 INSIGHTS FROM MYTHOLOGY

Devdutt Pattanaik

Illustrations by the author

An Imprint of HarperCollins*Publishers*

Indus Source Books
Indian Spirit, Universal Wisdom

First published in 2006 by Indus Source Books

This revised and updated edition
co-published in hardback in India in 2017 by Harper Element
An imprint of HarperCollins *Publishers* India
and
Indus Source Books

P-ISBN: 978-93-5264-497-1
E-ISBN: 978-93-5264-498-8

2 4 6 8 10 9 7 5 3 1

HarperCollins *Publishers*
A-75, Sector 57, Noida, Uttar Pradesh 201301, India
1 London Bridge Street, London, SE1 9GF, United Kingdom
Hazelton Lanes, 55 Avenue Road, Suite 2900, Toronto, Ontario M5R 3L2
and 1995 Markham Road, Scarborough, Ontario M1B 5M8, Canada
25 Ryde Road, Pymble, Sydney, NSW 2073, Australia
195 Broadway, New York, NY 10007, USA

Indus Source Books
PO Box 6194
Malabar Hill PO
Mumbai 400006
www.indussource.com

Typeset in Garamond by Special Effects, Mumbai

Printed and bound at
Thomson Press (India) Ltd.

Within infinite myths lies an eternal truth
But who sees it all?
Varuna has but a thousand eyes
Indra has a hundred
You and I, only two

Contents

Everybody tells a story

Storytelling is something that is very natural to human beings; we are constantly telling stories. Imagine a child coming home from school and telling his mother what happened there. What is he actually doing? He is telling a story of what happened in school, of how the teacher behaved, of how the students behaved, and as he narrates the story, villains appear, heroes appear, there is a plot and sometimes even a grand finale, where the good win and the bad are punished. The same happens when we pick up the phone for a chat. We want to tell a story or hear a story. We are all storytellers. We just don't realize it.

What is gossip if not storytelling? Some fact, some fiction, a lot of imagination. Newspapers are full of stories—events as seen by the reporter. Books are full of stories of plants and animals and planets. Shops are full of stories of products and brands and customers and advertising.

Usually, the word 'story' is used for fiction. We assume that when we narrate events from our life it is fact, not fiction. When we read about events in newspapers we assume they are fact, and hence not stories. 'Story' in common parlance then is the opposite of reality.

At a philosophical level, however, all that is narrated is story. What we call reality is actually the memory of an event seen filtered through our senses and our biases. At best, it is just a perception of what happened, one version of the truth; at worst, it is entirely the product of imagination. Once we understand this and accept this, we realize the power of storytelling. We realize that everything around us is a story—everything that we hear, see or remember stems from either perception or imagination.

Those who actually write a story are perhaps better storytellers than the rest of us because their stories appeal to a larger number of people, not to one or two as in a private conversation. They can enchant an audience, maybe an entire society, or a culture, or an entire generation, or maybe even several cultures over several generations.

It is very difficult to understand what makes any story special. Stories are like sweets that have an outer layer of toffee and a soft inner core of chocolate. As we eat this sweet, we first encounter the outer toffee. We chew on it, impatient to get to the chocolate within. The outer chewy part is the 'form' of the narrative and the inner chocolate core is the 'idea' of the narrative; the outer visible part is the flesh of the story (the plot, the characters, the tone, the pace) while the inner hidden part is the soul (the meaning).

The soul of a story is the reason why the story is being told. The soul can be just entertainment. All the storyteller wants to do is cause an adrenaline rush within you. In Sanskrit, adrenaline is known as rasa or mood juice. The storyteller is actually evoking the release of various kind of juices in his audience—there is shringar-rasa, to elicit the flow of romantic juices in the audience; and there is veer-rasa, where again through a series of stories, an event or actors, the storyteller is able to construct a heroic flavour in the mind of the audience. This is pure entertainment and there is no deeper level beyond that.

Sometimes, a story is just a report, with no desire to entertain. The storyteller here tries to be very dispassionate so as not to influence the judgement of the audience. Reportage is not easy because as humans we are quick to judge. The moment a storyteller talks about a fat woman, the audience instantly creates an image of a fat person in their head and if the audience does not like a fat person, even without a storyteller's intention, the fat woman becomes a negative character. If a storyteller describes a child as cute and cuddly then by the simple choice of words the image created in the audience's mind is something that delights. So it is very difficult to report without being judgemental. Journalists struggle to be unbiased but invariably succumb to judgement; even if they don't, the audience does, seeing meaning even where none exists.

Then there are stories with a clear strategic intent. It tells people what is good and what is bad. If the storyteller has a yardstick for deciding what is good and what is bad, heroes and villains are accordingly structured. When this is repeatedly done, it starts to influence the value system of those around. For example, if a storyteller believes that women are inferior to men, then their stories will be full of female characters who are cunning and manipulative and the male characters have to constantly survive their cunningness. Likewise, if a storyteller believes that women are victims, their stories will be full of female characters who are subjected to all forms of injustice. Storytellers then become creators of values and judgements, a feat that is rarely acknowledged.

Stories thus construct our truths—they tell us how to see the world. They construct villains and heroes. They tell us what romance is and how it feels when one is in love. They tell us how to behave when one is happy or unhappy. They tell us what good behaviour is and what bad behaviour is. Stories thus are and have always been a potent tool for political and cultural propaganda.

Parables are stories which very explicitly have a point of view. They sermonize. Parables all over the world are based on what a culture believes to be appropriate social conduct. On that count, a parable must be distinguished from a mythological narrative. Mythological narratives do not sermonize but they create the platform or framework that allows for sermonizing. While a parable can stand on its own, every mythological story is part of a larger whole. And so to understand a mythological story, we have to know all the other stories that make up the pieces of the jigsaw puzzle. Unlike parables, mythological stories are not focused on social issues—they seek to construct a bigger picture about the world. They attempt to explain why the world is the way it is, why the world came into being, what happens after we die. Typically, mythological narratives offer no solution but create a framework for other stories, parables included, which is why they play a rather profound role in any literature.

Traditional Western stories generally have a clear start and a clear finish. So the story typically begins with 'Once upon a time…' and ends with '…happily ever after'. But traditional Indian stories are rather different in structure. Take 'Vetal-Pachisi' for example. Vetal-Pachisi is a story of a king who repeatedly goes to a tree and pulls down a ghost with the intent to give him to a sorcerer. On the way, the ghost tells the king a story which ends with a question and he forces the king to answer the question. As soon as the answer is blurted out the ghost runs away from the king and returns to the tree. The king has to pull the ghost down again. This happens twenty-five times. Thus, the story always starts at the same point with pulling down the ghost and ends at the same point with the return of the ghost. The plot lies in between. The difference in structure of stories reflects the differences in cultural beliefs. The Western story celebrates a linear construct of life—with one beginning, one ending and one life in between. The Indian story celebrates a cyclical construct of life—with many beginnings, many endings and many lives in between. Thus, stories reflect the culture they emerge from, while reinforcing the culture at the same time.

Finally, stories have to be distinguished from narration. A story is basically a plot but narration is the process by which a story is told. The same story sounds different when the storyteller is different. And every storyteller changes his narration depending on the audience. All this makes storytelling rather complex, which is why our view of the world and our truths are also complex.

2

Gender bias in temples

Why were temples built in India? They did not always exist. Before temples, people worshipped rocks and rivers and stars: Kumbh Mela is a classic example of a Hindu ritual that does not involve any artificial structure. If one goes to the temple of Kamakhya in Assam or Vaishnodevi in Jammu, we realize that what is assumed to be a 'temple' is essentially a structure built around very simple natural rock formations. The structure then is the boundary that defines and delimits the sacred space around something very organic and natural. This creation of boundaries is the essence of patriarchy, for with boundaries come divisions and hierarchies that prop up the privileged. The physical boundaries express psychological boundaries that emerged long ago, before the structures, before gods and goddesses, in the earliest phases of civilization, when humanity emerged from the animal kingdom and sought meaning.

Every village of India is associated with grama-devis and grama-devas, often classified as fertility goddesses and guardian gods. The female divine provides and the male divine protects. For the female divine, the male minion is just a seed provider. Nothing more. The male divine protects the female divine. Sometimes he is also the seed provider. At other times, he is celibate like Hanuman, Bhairo baba and Aiyanar. Through celibacy these guardian gods express their respect for the Goddess, their mother. Celibacy, hence semen retention, also makes them powerful.

This notion of celibacy giving supernatural power gave rise to monastic orders. Monks sought to control the natural forces: the ability to walk on water or fly through air, the ability to change shape, be immortal. They also sought control over the mind: freedom from suffering, from fear. These accomplished ascetics (siddhas) shunned all things sensual, like the female temptresses (yoginis) who wandered in groups as matrikas and mahavidyas.

The Buddha created the earliest organized, institutionalized, monastic order in India. In his monasteries (viharas) women were not permitted. When they were, finally, they were forced to follow more rules than men, as they had not only to control their own desires, they also had to ensure they did not 'tempt' men. These viharas were built around chaityas which housed the stupa that contained a relic of the Buddha. These were the first grand structures of India, carved into rocks. Before that, shrines (devalayas) of fertility goddesses and guardian gods existed only under trees, beside rivers and inside caves, unrestrained by artificial walls and roofs.

Temples of stone were built to counter Buddhist thought by highlighting the joys of household life. Temple walls and temple customs expressed song and dance and food and pleasure. The enshrined deities got married in grand ceremonies (as in Brahmotsavam in Tirupati). They were taken care of by priests and temple dancers. These complexes were a far cry from the serenity and silence of the vihara. They celebrated power and pleasure and beauty on a grand scale. But like Buddhist monasteries, these temples were controlled by men, the Brahmins. When the devadasis became too powerful, they were kicked out by being declared 'prostitutes', with a little help from the British.

Ironically today, temples—that embodiment of household life—are controlled by Hindu monks (mahants). Celibacy is seen as the hallmark of religiosity and purity, and embodied in celibate, women-shunning deities such as Shani and Ayyappa. In ashrams of modern-day gurus, male sanyasis are called 'swami' or master, while female sanyasis are called 'maa' or mother, thus endorsing the traditional roles of man as protector and proprietor and woman as procreator and provider.

Is celibacy a sign of respect for women, or just a clever form of misogyny? Why do the guardian gods, gurus, monks and male devotees shun the feminine? Is it to retain their semen, hence gaining supernatural powers, a common belief in tantric texts? Or is it because they want to purify themselves, and so stay away from pollutants, such as menstruating women? These are popular ideas (Traditional beliefs? Superstitions?) that most activists do not want to engage with, for it will open a huge can of worms.

We prefer the sterility of neo-Vedanta popularized by male-dominated monastic Hindu 'missions' in the early twentieth century, where God has no gender, or sexuality, hence looks upon men and women equally. Women breaking into men-only temples may be dramatic, like the storming of the Bastille, but it does not challenge the patriarchal psychology that makes 'celibacy' purifying and 'sexuality' polluting.

3

Caste again

 ny discussion of caste is politically volatile. For centuries it denied millions basic human dignity, even water. Yet, caste remains a pan-Indian reality, percolating beyond the Hindu fold. One wonders how sages who spoke of the Atma, the divine soul in all living creatures, could also institute such a cruel system. It makes no sense!

But when one delves deeper, one notices something very significant. The sages who discussed the caste system were also firm believers in rebirth. Studying caste in isolation, without considering rebirth, creates a myopic understanding of the subject.

What distinguishes Hinduism from most other religions of the world is belief in rebirth. A newborn then is an old soul wrapped in a new flesh, its caste being determined by karmic baggage. In the absence of the rebirth lens, the caste system gives unfair advantages to one set of children over another. For believers of the one-life paradigm, all children are born equal, either in sin (if one believes in the Fall from Eden) or with genetic differences (if one believes in science). Appreciating this difference is critical.

The 'origin' of caste is conventionally traced to the 'Purusha Sukta' hymn of the Rig Veda, according to which society is an organism whose head, hands, thighs/trunk and feet are made of those involved in ritual, administration, trade and service. This was the varna system which later metamorphosed, due to a variety of reasons, into the jati system, based on various professions. Jati was determined by birth. Jati could not be changed, even by marriage.

But for the rishis who sang the 'Purusha Sukta', caste had no 'origin' as it was timeless. Caste, it was believed, ensured a model social organization that ensured predictability. Every child knew his role in society at birth itself. This role changed in past and future lives. A priest in this life could be a trader in another and a farmer in yet another. This was made explicit in the story of Vishnu's avatars. In one avatar God is a priest (Vaman), in another he is a king (Rama) and in another he is a cowherd/charioteer (Krishna). The point to be noted here is that each role/caste mattered in that lifetime. Nothing was superior or inferior. Every caste was just different.

How then did the caste system become hierarchical and draconian? The Left blames the Brahmins for it. The Right comes up with apologetic explanations involving corruption over time due to foreign incursions. Perhaps this has something to do with a culture turning away from the faith in rebirth.

If people continued to believe in rebirth, the Dalit would not be treated as he was and continues to be even today. If one believed that current caste privileges were the result of merits earned in past life, then one would not spend this life exhausting merit. One would instead focus on accumulating merit. Merit is accumulated by acts of human empathy and compassion and kindness. That exploitation and indifference and even cruelty, not empathy, mark the caste system, indicates a decline of faith in the notion of rebirth.

The rishis celebrated the notion of rebirth perhaps to provoke empathy. If this life influences the next life, one would be kinder, maybe. But if this is the one and only life, why should one be kind? While one-life cultures used the God–Devil binary to inject empathy into human behaviour, rebirth cultures used the karmic balance sheet to do the same. Even divinity is subject to karma and caste in rebirth cultures, which is why every avatar of Vishnu is associated with a caste.

Both in the Mahabharata and in the Ramayana, Brahmins are killed for taking advantage of their privileged positions. In the Mahabharata, Krishna encourages the beheading of Drona who, rather than staying a priest, used his knowledge of warfare to make his own son king. In the Ramayana, Rama kills Ravana who, though born in a family of priests, uses military might to terrorize the world. In caste-ridden India, Brahma-hatya or killing of the Brahmin was the worst of sins. Yet, we find these stories of God committing Brahma-hatya-paap for the sake of dharma.

Jain traditions say that in a future life, Ravana will become a Tirthankara. In other words, the villain who abused his caste privileges will finally understand the point of it all and attain enlightenment. He will develop a line of sight that extends beyond his current life to include his other lives in other lifetimes. When faith in rebirth is internalized completely, empathy has to bloom. For then we realize that all souls are interconnected. To hurt the other is to hurt the self, if not in this lifetime, then in the next.

4

Cultural roots of evil

The English word 'evil' cannot be translated in any Indian language. There is no synonym of evil in Hindi or Tamil. And yet, when this is pointed out, everyone feels odd. They keep offering alternative words that mean evil. Surely evil exists!

A few years ago the Dalai Lama said that there is goodness in all human beings, even in Hitler. This idea annoyed and irritated many in the West. How can anyone say anything good about Hitler? Someone once tried to say that the punishment against actor Shiney Ahuja was too harsh. He was silenced with the rhetoric: How can anyone speak in favour of a rapist?

Evil means the absence of good. Implicit in the word 'evil' is a religious concept. It means the absence of God. In the Bhagavad Gita, Krishna says that everything that exists is a manifestation of the divine. And so nothing can be devoid of . divinity. And so nothing can be evil.

Most Indians believe in rebirth and the theory of karma. As a result, every event is the outcome of some past deed. Even the worst of events can be explained by karma. In one Purana, for example, there is a story of Sita accidentally killing one of a pair of lovebirds and so being cursed by the surviving bird that she too would be separated from her beloved. In another Purana, Vishnu, the preserver of the world, beheads the mother of a sage, Kavya, who attempts to help the asuras. For this action Vishnu is cursed that he will descend on earth in human form and experience death. Thus, even God is subject to the laws of karma. When everything is karmic, the notion of evil is not needed to make sense of a terrible action. That is why in Indian languages there is no concept or word for evil.

All this makes evil a cultural concept, not a universal one. The rational discourse aligns itself with the 'evil' discourse and justifies the existence of evil through words like 'psychopath' and 'sociopath' whose usage has shot up in American crime-based television series like *CSI* or *Dexter*. It stems from a clear need to justify killing of the undesirable. Basically, what we are being told is that there are human beings on this planet who do not deserve mercy or pity. Like the Orcs of the Lord of the Rings trilogy, we are being told they have to be killed. We cannot live with them.

In India, the word 'evil' is being replaced by the word 'corrupt'. Increasingly, influenced by Western religious, political and social discourses, Indians are beginning to believe that the way to create a better world is by getting rid of 'evil' politicians and 'evil' bureaucrats and 'evil' businessmen using lawful and, if necessary, lawless means. This is a dangerous trend. It means that we have stopped looking at people as human beings who can be heroes or villains in different situations. Instead we have chosen to box all humans as good and evil, boxes from which there is no escape.

There seems to be an urgency to declare people as evil or corrupt and no urgency whatsoever to reflect on what makes people evil or corrupt. Refusal to reflect indicates an arrogance that we already know. And that certainly is a dangerous trend.

5

Look left and right

Every time I use the words 'Indian mythology', some people say I should write 'Hindu mythology'. And when I call the Mahabharata a Hindu epic, I am told it should be called an Indian epic. Then I seek clarification, 'Is the Ramayana a Hindu epic or an Indian epic?' Prompt comes the reply, 'Hindu, of course.'

So now I am confused. What is Indian and what is Hindu? Are they mutually exclusive? Should I call the Taj Mahal an Indian monument or a Muslim mausoleum? Should I call Mother Teresa an Indian or a Christian? What is the correct terminology? What should a qualification include or exclude? What is the right word that will not offend anyone? Whose permission should I take? The lawyers, the religious leaders, the politicians, the bureaucrats, the anti-corruption brigade, the leftists, the rightists or the secularists?

Gradually, India is becoming more a political terminology and less a cultural and geographic one. Gradually, secularism is turning into another religion, with a god called logic, rules that need to be followed and prophets who bark if you do not align to the rules or submit to logic.

Every religion has a positive side that teaches love and inclusion, and a horrible side that celebrates hatred and exclusion. Secularism is following the same trend. Ostensibly it was created to love and include, but all it seems to be doing is fuel hate and exclusion. You are excluded if you do not follow a secular agenda and secular rules. If you wear a religious symbol, a veil or a teeka or a cross, you become instantly untouchable and branded a potential terrorist. It is scary!

Look beneath the surface and the problem is neurological. Our brain has two halves—the left half and the right half. The left half is more analytical and the right half is more abstract. From the left comes science and from the right comes arts. From the left comes politics and from the right comes romance. The left half functions by exclusion, and tends to be more focused. The right half functions by inclusion, and tends to be more diffused. It seems the world is shifting more towards the left and rejecting the right, preferring science to art, politics to romance, excluding to including.

As children we were told, 'Look left, then right, and then cross the road.' The leftists look only left, the rightists look only right and the secularists look only straight ahead.

Accidents then are bound to happen. Accidents do happen, but as the left walks left and the right walks right and the secularist walks straight, each one smug and self-righteous, no one turns around to see the devastation in their wake.

Perhaps that is why the ancient rishis visualized Brahma as the four-headed god who has a head for the left and a head for the right and a head in front and a head behind. Only then can we see it all, try and make as much room as we can for everything and everyone, not bristle and rave and rant when Christian sages and Muslim monuments and Hindu epics are qualified as Indian. Only when we include will the world be a better place.

6

Frames of reference

Everybody sees the world through a frame of reference. No one but the gods has the full picture. At least that is what the following tale from Hindu mythology seeks to communicate:

All the gods of the Hindu pantheon once went to Mount Kailas to pay their respects to Shiva, the destroyer. Brahma, the creator, came first on his goose, followed by Indra, the rain god, on his elephant and Agni, the fire god, on his goat. Chandra, the moon god, came riding his antelope. Vishnu, the guardian of the world, flew in on his eagle, the mighty Garuda. Yama, the god of death, was the last to arrive, delayed as usual by his mount, a buffalo. Garuda noticed that before entering Kailas, Yama's eyes fell on a tiny sparrow that had perched itself on a ledge near the gate, chirping a welcome song for all the gods. Yama frowned and crinkled his brow before shrugging his shoulders and joining the gods. Garuda, who was king of all birds, concluded that the days of the sparrow were numbered. Why else would the god of death frown on seeing it? Perhaps the sparrow would die of starvation on the cold, icy slopes of Kailas. Garuda looked at the little bird—so young, innocent, eager to see the world. Overwhelmed with parental affection, Garuda took a decision to keep the little sparrow out of Yama's heartless reach. Taking the bird in the palms of his hands, he flew across seven hills and seven rivers until he reached the forest of Dandaka. There in the hermitage of a sage called Pippalada he found a mango tree. 'The sparrow will be safe here,' he said to himself. He built a nest on the mango tree, left the sparrow there and returned to Kailas, pleased with himself. Soon the gathering of the gods drew to a close. The gods began to leave: Brahma on his goose, Indra on his elephant, Agni on his goat, Chandra on his antelope. Vishnu came out along with Yama. At the gate, Yama turned to look at the ledge where he had seen the singing sparrow. Finding it empty, he smiled. Vishnu asked Yama, 'Why are you smiling?' Yama answered, 'When I was entering Kailas I saw this sparrow here that was destined to die today, eaten by a python that lives in the mango tree that grows in the hermitage of Sage Pippalada in the forest of Dandaka, which as you know is far away. I wondered how the sparrow would travel the distance in a day. I was worried about all the repercussions that might follow if the bird did not die at the appointed hour in the appointed place. But somehow things have gone as planned

and my accounts book is balanced. That is why I am smiling.'
Vishnu divined what had happened and turned to Garuda.
Garuda, who had overheard the conversation, did not know
what to feel.

For the python, Garuda is the giver of food. For the
sparrow, Garuda is the taker of life. But after Yama speaks,
Garuda is nothing but an instrument of fate, part of a grand
narrative not of his own making.

It is possible to narrate the story differently, without
Yama and his accounts book. In such a story, Garuda's
spontaneous act of kindness goes horribly wrong because
of the unfortunate coincidence of the python's presence. In
this story, the frame of reference is free will.

It is also possible to add a twist to this story. Garuda prays
to Shiva for help and Shiva rescues the sparrow from the jaws
of death and restores it to the safety of Kailas, overriding the
accounts book of Yama. In this story, the frame of reference
is God, who is greater than the gods.

Fate. Free will. God. Three frames of reference that have
sustained cultures for centuries. Three frames of reference
that can never be proved or disproved. Three frames of
reference that have to be believed. And when believed, can
help individuals and communities thrive.

The Greeks sought Truth using reason: an understanding
of the world that when argued at any time, at any place,
yielded the same result. This was logos. Logic. Rationality.
It gave birth to science and mathematics. It revealed how
people are 'actually' born and how the sun 'actually' rises.

It took man to the moon. But it never gave the reason why man exists on earth in the first place.

Science tell us 'how', not 'why'. Explanations can never ever be solutions. Individuals need solutions. Cultures need solutions. A solution to the conundrum called life. A solution that gives meaning and purpose, tools to cope with crises, justify ambition and build communities. One has no choice but to withdraw into constructed realities, cling to a frame of reference, any frame of reference with all its inherent limitations. There is no escape from myth.

Myths are however not tangible. To experience the idea of fate, free will or God, one needs stories, symbols and rituals—language that is heard, seen and performed. The story of Garuda, for example, depending on the version chosen, helps establish the myth of fate, free will or God in the Hindu mind space. The body of stories, symbols and rituals that communicates a myth to a people is called mythology. All cultures—Hindu, Christian, Greek or American—are guided by a myth communicated through a mythology.

When myths and mythologies of cultures are compared with one another, there are bound to be similarities and dissimilarities. Similarities reflect the humanity of a culture, dissimilarities its uniqueness. Hindus and Buddhists are similar in that they both believe in the wheel of rebirth, but they are dissimilar in that only Hindus believe in the concept of the eternal, unchanging soul. Hindus and Muslims are similar in that they both accept God as being all-powerful, but they are dissimilar in that Muslims believe in one life and one way of reaching God, by following the path revealed to Prophet Muhammad.

It has been mankind's endeavour to find a common understanding for the world, a common frame of reference, a common myth—a uniform civil code. This may not be possible, as it would mean getting all of humanity to look at life through the same window and no other. An irrational window at that.

Any attempt to communicate myth rationally is doomed to failure. There are always questions that can challenge the discourse of fate, free will and God. In all cultures, therefore, mythology is far removed from reality and rationality: gods with three heads, demons with eight arms, virgin births, parting seas, promised lands, sacraments of fire and covenants of blood. This indifference to logic ensures myth is not reasoned with, but accepted unconditionally through a suspension of disbelief.

For the believer, myth is real. It makes rational sense. It cannot be argued with. It is sacred. This allows the myth to be communicated across generations and geography without distortion. Myth, however, is not static. Just as it informs history and geography, it is informed by history and geography. This is why beliefs and customs change over time. There was a time when people believed only members of a particular caste could enter a shrine. This belief is no longer encouraged. Myth once said that people were unequal. Myth now says that all people are equal. Yesterday the inequality of people was real. Today the equality of people is real.

We forget that human life is not governed by logic. Emotions that drive humanity—love, hate, fear, greed, ambition—cannot be rationalized. Human beings therefore cannot make sense of life through scientific, evidence-based discourses. For the sake of survival and sanity, they need to believe in a frame of reference. They need myth. And myth needs mythology.

7

Changing patterns

Every morning, in my neighbourhood, find a woman painting pretty patterns using rice-flour paste just outside the door of her house. She is from Andhra Pradesh and she calls it muggu. This practice is seen in millions of households across India, mostly in the south, where it is also called kolam. The patterns extend beyond the doorway to the walls of the house too. It is called alpana in Odisha and Bengal, aripan in Bihar, rangoli in Maharashtra. Once, this was a daily practice. In many parts of rural India it is still so. But in most parts of India, this practice is restricted to festival time, Diwali being the most popular one. Other times are Kojagari, the full moon before Diwali; and Krishna Janmashtami, the birth of Krishna. These patterns are also seen during weddings. This practice of decorating the threshold is even seen in Parsi households.

The patterns are done only by women. The material used was once rice flour but now synthetic powders, even paint, are increasingly being used. And for the busy households there are ready-made bright sticker rangolis.

Does this have any logical purpose? Yes, according to the rationalists, who say the rice flour is meant to feed ants so they do not enter the house. Does it have any aesthetic purpose? Yes, it enables the homemakers to make the house pretty. But that still does not explain why it has to be done every day, by women, at the doorway. That the practice becomes elaborate during festivals and rites of passage indicates that this ritual is rooted in emotion, myth and magic.

In all probability these are talismans, bringing good luck into the household. This was a ritual where the matriarch of the household was the grand priestess. This is how she harnessed cosmic energy and brought it into the household. This is how she anchored divine grace to the house. This was a ritual that she did on her own, without the support of any men or priests. But to do this, there were rules. She had to be a married woman with children. Widows were not allowed to do this and virgins could only support their mothers. Male priests were allowed to make a rangoli, but only as part of a ritual; the rangoli was used to mark out the sacred space where the rituals were performed. This was different from the woman's rangoli that transformed the house into a sacred space.

Many are of the opinion that the rangoli or kolam is what later transformed into tantric mandalas and yantras. Or maybe the process was the other way around. These mandalas and yantras used geometrical forms to represent various gods and goddesses, various natural spirits. A downward pointing triangle represented woman; an upward pointing triangle represented man. A circle represented nature while a square represented culture. A lotus represented the womb. A pentagram represented Venus and the five elements.

Typically, a rangoli begins with a grid of dots being made. The more the dots, the more elaborate the patterns. Given the same grid, different women would see different patterns in it and draw accordingly. So if one walked down the village street, one would find numerous households with varying patterns.

Different households were run by different women and each woman had her own identity and her own sense of aesthetics, which she expressed each day in her rangoli. While the grid of dots united them all, as did the ritual of making the rangoli, the specific pattern reminded all of the differences. Every woman did her best but no one compared or tried to turn it into a competition. The point was not to be better than others but to be the best one could be, for one's own house. Through these beautiful but different patterns, generations of Indians were taught to be tolerant, to enjoy other people's patterns and one's own, without being judgemental.

Just by looking at the pattern one could determine the mood of the household. Daily patterns indicated discipline. Beautiful patterns indicated joy. Elaborate patterns indicated focus and dedication. Shoddy patterns indicated a bad mood, maybe a fight the previous night. Absence of a pattern meant something was amiss in the household. The kolam serves almost as a message board of the household.

Once in a while the patterns were fixed, as during festival times. Then the women had to set individual creativity aside and align to the demands of culture or tradition. Those were the days when the women were part of a larger whole. The village rules became household rules.

The rangoli was never permanent. It was wiped off each morning, reminding all that things change. Yesterday's bad mood can become tomorrow's good mood. Bad patterns can give way to good patterns. The household changes and so do its patterns. People learn and grow and with that, patterns become more confident and more joyful.

8

Baby on the banyan leaf

Markandeya was no ordinary sage. He had been blessed with immortality. Perhaps so that he could see and report what no one else had seen. Only he witnessed pralaya and lived to tell its tale.

Pralaya means the end of the world. Hindus believe that just as plants die, animals die, humans die and so does the world. The moment of the death of the world is marked by the rising of the oceans. Waters rise to submerge the continents and the mountains, drowning every forest and river valley and desert and island. Nothing survives this great deluge. Markandeya witnessed this sight and was filled with fear. But the waters did not pull Markandeya down. He stayed afloat mysteriously.

Then Markandeya saw a strange sight. He saw a banyan leaf cradled by the waves. On it he saw a radiant baby gurgling happily, sucking his right big toe. The child inhaled deeply. Markandeya found himself being sucked into the baby's body through his nostril. Within, to Markandeya's surprise, was the whole world, all the realms, the lokas that stand above the sky and the talas that are located below the earth. Surrounding these realms were oceans. In these realms were mountains and rivers and forests and all types of living creatures—plants, animals, humans, devas, asuras, nagas, yakshas, rakshasas, apsaras, gandharvas. It was as if pralaya had never happened. Everyone lived as they did before, oblivious of the great calamity outside the child's body.

Markandeya then found himself being exhaled out. He was back in the waters, surrounded by the waves, watching the baby gurgling happily on the banyan leaf. He realized he was being given a message, a silent symbolic message. It was up to him to decipher it.

Outside the baby's body was death, inside was life. As long as Markandeya was outside, he experienced fear and insecurity, within he experienced wonder and security. And the baby simply gurgled, unafraid and confident, fully aware that life and death were two aspects of life, rising and falling like waves in an unending ocean. The baby was God who saw the events as they were, without expectation or prejudice, unlike Markandeya.

Markandeya realized that pralaya is both real and metaphorical, objective and subjective, marking the moment when everything collapses around us, all structures break down and nothing exists to support us, when we are left with nothing to hold on to. The only thing that can take us through, like a raft, like the banyan leaf afloat on the waves, is our faith. Faith in what? Faith in an entity that defies all change and transformation. Not everyone may have experienced this spiritual reality, but everyone can imagine it. It is a state where there is no death, no change, no restlessness—only stillness, silence, serenity and immortality. This is represented in sacred art as the banyan tree, which is why it is referred to as the akshaya (indestructible) vat (fig).

That God takes the form of a baby is a marker of renewal and innocence. The world collapses when innocence and purity is lost; it will be reborn once again, fresh and innocent. Why was the baby sucking his big toe? In the 'Purusha Sukta' hymn of the Rig Veda, Markandeya knew, society is defined as a living, breathing creature (Purusha) and not an impersonal organization. The head was constituted by Brahmins (philosophers), the arms by Kshatriyas (warriors), the trunk by Vaishyas (traders) and the feet by Shudras (labourers). Wisdom is celebrating the whole body, especially the neglected feet. The innocent baby loves the foot and suckles on it. It does not see the feet as inferior or dirty or inauspicious. Such judgements are cultural; a child has no clue about them. Society creates values that result in one group of people justifying their domination over, and suppression of, another group of people. Society creates values where the head is celebrated and feet exploited and ignored. When this happens, society collapses and pralaya follows.

What is also significant is that the right big toe is being suckled and not the left big toe. In symbolic terms, the left side of the body, which is the side of the heart, is associated with material reality and the right side is associated with spiritual reality. The baby looks at the spiritual side of things. He knows that differences between philosophers, warriors, traders and labourers are just superficial, of the mind and matter, of the flesh and social station. These are temporary and contextual. What is common and permanent in all of them is the soul, the spiritual reality that lives in the flesh of all those who inhabit society, from the highest to the lowest, the richest to the poorest and the strongest to the weakest. Within every flesh is divinity. The fool focuses on the flesh, the wise focus on the soul. The fool therefore will encounter pralaya outside divinity; the wise will always enjoy tranquility inside divinity.

9

Botox for the waning moon

Imagine if the moon never waned. I guess then we would not celebrate Kojagari or Kartik Poornima or Sharad Poornima on full-moon nights. And lovers would not sing songs equating the moon's phases with the mood swings of their beloved. We would not have 'Id ka Chand' or 'Chaudhvin ka Chand' or 'Ganesh Chaturthi'.

I wonder why our ancestors insisted on having a calendar based on the moon. Is there a message there? All things that wax eventually wane. All things that wane eventually wax. In Jain mythology, there is the concept of the world going through phases like the moon, 'Sushama Sushama' representing boom times, the full moon, and 'Dushama Dushama' representing bust times, the new moon. Not surprising, since the Jain community have been traders for centuries and have understood, unlike modern management and business consultants, that market forces shift over time and are never permanent.

The story goes that Brahma in the form of Daksha had twenty-seven daughters, the nakshatras. He gave them in marriage to Chandra, the moon god. Chandra loved only one of the wives and so spent all his time with her, annoying the other wives who complained to Daksha. Daksha insisted that Chandra treat all his wives equally. 'I can't,' said Chandra. 'The heart cannot be controlled by rules.' Angry, Daksha cursed Chandra with the wasting disease, causing him to wane. Just when he was about to disappear, Chandra was advised to pray to Shiva, the hermit god, who had given Sanjivani Vidya or the science of regeneration to the asuras, because of which the asuras could always be resurrected after being killed by devas. Chandra prayed to Shiva and Shiva offered him a place on his forehead. Contact with Shiva's forehead enabled Chandra to wax once again.

From that day on, Shiva came to be known as Chandrashekhar, one whose head is adorned by the crescent waning moon. Chandra is called Soma, which means the elixir of regeneration. Shiva is therefore also known as Somnath. As a reminder of the god who helped the moon wax and so can help regenerate life and bring back fortune once again into our lives, Shiva is worshipped on the fourteenth lunar day of every waxing half. This is the Shiva-ratri, the most important of which is the Maha-Shiva-ratri that falls at the start of spring.

Chandra, they say, moves from one wife to another every night. He waxes when he comes closer to his favourite,

Rohini. He wanes when he moves away from her. On full-moon nights, he is with her. On new-moon nights, he is away from every wife. Thus the waxing and waning moon is a metaphor for romantic mood as well as virility.

If youth is the waxing phase and old age the waning phase, when will we wax again? Next life? That's a myth, isn't it? We don't believe in rebirth, soul or God, even if we clutch the Gita every night (just in case). We want to resist the waning process in this life. We want yoga and facelifts and hair-weaving to perk us up. Unfortunately, gravity will always pull us down. We fight back. We get touchy when we are called 'old'. We snap, '*Your* father is old.' Well, fathers usually are. Especially when sons grow up and have children of their own. It feels good to imagine grandchildren playing with wrinkles, rather than Botox-drenched tissues. In some societies, it is noble to wane with grace.

Timeless wisdom of the horse

The spiritual wisdom of India, based on the idea of rebirth, is called sanatan, which means timeless and universal, wisdom that cannot be restricted to sthana, kala, patra, geography, history or people. So to call it Indian wisdom or Hindu wisdom is not quite appropriate. Something that is timeless and universal cannot be restricted to India or Indians alone. To do so is being rather chauvinistic; the temptation of possessive nouns and pronouns is perhaps too great to resist.

The following story best explains the relationship of India, Indians and sanatan: Unable to bear his poverty, a priest went to the temple and begged the deity there for a solution. That night the deity left a golden pot in the courtyard of the priest's house. The priest found the golden pot with some water in it. He threw the water out and went to the market where he sold the pot to a merchant. With the money he received, he repaid all his debts and returned home a rich man laden with gifts for his family. Soon after, his family fought over the vast wealth, everyone from his wife to his children to his parents and his siblings demanding their share. Unable to bear the mental agony, the priest went back to the temple and complained to the deity, 'You have added to my problem, not solved it with the golden pot.' And the deity said, 'Golden pot? What golden pot? I gave you the elixir of contentment, enough for you and your family. It happened to be contained in a golden pot. Did you not drink it?'

The priest represents the Indian, the golden pot represents India and the elixir of contentment represents the wisdom called sanatan. Yes, sanatan did flourish in the Indian subcontinent. But no, all Indians have not consumed it; otherwise Indians would be the most content and affectionate people in the world. Proximity to sanatan, however, has had its benefits. It has shaped the Indian way and made Indians more comfortable with adjustment, ambiguity, reflection, introspection and uncertainty.

Why did sanatan flourish only in the Indian subcontinent? We will never really know. We can only speculate. Below is a rather uncommon speculation.

Though not native to India, the horse is a much-revered animal for Indians, sacrificed during the Ashwamedha yagna in ancient times and worshipped as the horse-headed deity, Hayagriva, since medieval times. We even find votive offerings of horse terracotta images being offered down south.

All through history, people have entered India on horse

carts and horseback from the mountain passes of the north-west, but have never left. These include the Mughals, and the Huns before them, and the Greeks and Persians before them, and before them countless nameless cattle-herding tribes. This has been going on for so long that in many cases, we have no memory. No one can explain how this one subcontinent has so many languages, some with Indo-European roots, some with Dravidian roots and some (dialects from the tribal areas of Jharkhand) that can even be traced to Austro-African roots.

The horse riders entered a fertile land watered by many rivers: the Sindhu (Indus), Ganga, Narmada, Krishna, Kaveri and the now-dry Saraswati, to name a few. The land was rich enough to feed every nomad. And so, after an initial period of conflict, every nomad settled down as a farmer with other farmers. This happened again and again, generation after generation, over thousands of years.

While the nomadic body settled, the nomadic mind continued to wander to the starry skies, through still mountains and the flowing rivers, to clouds bearing the uncertain rain. They sought meaning, reconciling the memories of scarcity that drives a nomad and the reality of abundance on the Indian riverbanks.

The land kept making room for every new nomad. And the people kept making room for every idea, rejecting nothing, creating a pattern that could include all ideas and accommodate every view of life. The only way to make room for everyone was to come up with the idea of multiple lives, rebirth, karma. Thus, sanatan came into being.

The Europeans were the only ones to come into India, keep a studied distance and then leave. And they have encouraged many Indians to reject the sanatan way of thinking. They were obsessed with objectivity, absoluteness and exclusion of others. This scientific thinking has created engineer-minds that have flattened the world with wealth, technology and the Internet, creating a global village: a peculiar village where everyone is actually a nomad, chasing careers or bungee-jumping or surfing the Internet, constantly searching for something. It is a world where everyone argues and everyone wants to be right. It is a world where the haves reject the have-nots and the have-nots reject the haves.

The farmer-mind waits and watches. He has made room for English and TV and the Internet and MTV. But he knows that the old ways also have value. The new nomad is a tough one to be accommodated but has to eventually. Both the old and the new have to make room for each other. The left and the right are equally valid. As he sees everyone wanting to save the world with a sense of urgency, their way, rejecting other ways, he wonders: When will they realize that the human mind is wide enough to accommodate all ways of thinking? People will arrive at this conclusion in time.

Eventually, as always, the horse-mind will bring the nomad-mind back into India through the mountain passes of the West! It will allow itself to be sacrificed as during the ancient Ashwamedha rituals, so that there is no return to scarcity. It will allow itself to be worshipped as Hayagriva as one who brings people into abundance.

11

Immersion time

Every year, when it is time for the monsoon to wane, his image is brought home, bedecked and fed and worshipped with incense and flowers and lamps for ten days, and then immersed in the sea. This is done again and again, every year, the inviting of the god and then bidding him goodbye with such concrete efficiency. Every year we see the clay idols being set up and every year, following the fourteenth day of the waxing moon, we see the remains of the majestic idols in the sea. Ten days of festivities and music and dance and prayer, and then silence. Time to worship the ancestors.

The following fortnight will be devoted to the dead. This is the fortnight for the Pitris, a time to remember and reassure them that their rebirth is imminent.

A fundamental concept that governs religions that originated in India is 'everything ends'. Nothing lasts forever. The inanimate is transformed into different forms. The animate has to die. Death, change, transformation govern nature. It is the only thing that is predictable. Life is about coping with this change. The inanimate rock and river, the nir-jiva, are not aware of death and so do not resist change. Animate plants and animals, the sa-jiva, are aware of death and so resist dying; running and fighting as they struggle to survive. Humans alone are blessed with wondering about death, seeking meaning in life, desperately wanting to know: What is the point of it all? Nature offers no answers. Religions seem to offer hypotheses. Even science has raised its hands in despair. No one really knows. And that is frustrating. So we choose to ignore existentialist angst and devote ourselves to some silly plan, a goal or mission of our own making that we declare to be the purpose of our life.

In the Mahabharata, Yudhishthira, when asked by the Yaksha to identify the greatest wonder in the world, states, 'Every day people die and the rest live as if they are immortal. That is the greatest wonder.'

Every year Ganesha is dunked into the sea. Gradually the clay dissolves into the water. His image disappears. Was this an elaborate ritual designed by our ancestors to draw attention to the ephemeral nature of life? Nothing lasts forever. The point of life is then not to achieve something, but to sit and wonder what the point of it all is. That is why India is renowned for its sages and mystics and philosophers. What mattered more for us was not the external material achievements but the inner spiritual realizations—wisdom that no one can pass on like wealth, but has to be ignited individually. Wisdom makes us kinder, gentler, humbler, not angry revolutionaries—for every revolution will also die, eventually, inevitably.

We often forget that Lakshmi and Saraswati accompany Ganesha. When Ganesha arrives, Lakshmi walks in our direction. When Ganesha leaves, Saraswati walks in our direction. With both comes a goddess: wealth in boom time, wisdom in bust time. Lakshmi makes us grow externally, whether we want to or not. Saraswati helps us grow internally, but only if we allow her to. There is clearly a preference for one goddess over the other. And Ganesha smiles, for he has faith in humanity, and infinite patience.

12

Krishna's best friend

 Krishna had a friend called Uddhava, a cousin just like Arjuna, the Pandava. While Arjuna was the son of Kunti, Vasudeva's sister, Uddhava was the son of Devabhaga, Vasudeva's brother. Born and raised in Mathura, Uddhava was a great intellectual, educated by Brihaspati, the guru of the devas. He was amongst the first Yadavas to befriend Krishna when the latter was brought by Kamsa to Mathura from Vrindavan. In some traditions, Uddhava grew up with Krishna in Vrindavan.

The two could not be more different from each other. Uddhava was raised in the city; Krishna was raised in a village of cowherds. Uddhava was educated; Krishna was uneducated. Uddhava was a serious scholar of the scriptures; Krishna was a charming rake. Uddhava silently suffered Kamsa's excesses; Krishna overthrew Kamsa and became a rebel and hero. Though opposites, Uddhava had the wisdom to realize that Krishna was no ordinary soul; he was special. And Krishna saw in Uddhava a seeker, a genuine student, not a smug academician.

Uddhava is famous for two major events. In one, he is asked to go to Vrindavan and convey to the milkmaids there that Krishna, contrary to the promise he had made, would never, ever be coming back. In the other, he has to go to Dwaraka and inform everyone there that the Yadava clan has been destroyed and Krishna is dead. Both events are associated with separation, pain and death. While Uddhava is the beneficiary in the first event (Krishna comes to him), he is the victim in the other (Krishna leaves him).

When Uddhava goes to Vrindavan, the eager and anxious milkmaids mistake him for Krishna, for he comes in the same chariot that took Krishna away and, as Krishna's cousin, he has similar features. But then they realize, Uddhava is no Krishna. He does not know how to comfort. He does not know how to be emotional. He is calm and composed like a priest, passing on the news with accuracy, not understanding why the women wail like children.

Uddhava advises the gopikas to read the scriptures that speak of how the world is full of change and suffering and how the wise detach themselves from worldly things. The milkmaids, led by Radha, lash back. This forms the basis of the famous 'Bhramar Gita', song of the bee, where the milkmaids equate themselves with the flower that is left behind by the bee after being drained of nectar and fragrance. Krishna, the bee, has moved on to another land, to other women, to other flowers. They do not resent him or wish him to change the course of his life but they want the right to pine for him. This is viraha bhakti, devotion born of separation. Uddhava offers them knowledge to console them, but the women say, 'We do not want to be consoled. Where do we put your knowledge? Every being of ours is occupied by memories of Krishna!' Uddhava, the intellectual, returns humbled by the unconditional love of the milkmaids. The gyan yogi understands the bhakti yogi for the first time.

Life moves on. Uddhava watches Krishna take the Yadavas out of Mathura to Dwaraka. He watches him help the Pandavas win the war against the Kauravas. In the final chapter of Krishna's life, a great civil war breaks out amongst the Yadavas. And Krishna does nothing to stop his kinsmen from killing each other. Then a hunter's poisoned arrow strikes Krishna on the sole of his left foot. Uddhava is aghast, while Krishna calmly requests him to convey the message of his demise to the women, children and aged people, his old father included, and the news of the great tragic end of the clan. 'How can you be so calm?' asks Uddhava. In response, Krishna says with a smile, 'Why? Are you not detached?' He then reveals to his friend the 'Uddhava Gita' also known as the 'Hamsa Gita', the song of the goose.

Uddhava realizes that he is very knowledgeable but not quite wise. He knows every verse of every scripture, every argument and counter-argument, but when it comes to coping with reality he is no different from the milkmaids whose wailing he frowned upon. And unlike Radha, he does not know how to accept and let go. 'If you truly have wisdom, Uddhava,' says Krishna, 'you will have faith and patience.'

Faith means truly accepting that material things are bound to go, but not spiritual things. Krishna will leave Vrindavan eventually, Krishna will leave Mathura and Dwaraka inevitably, but Vishnu's Vaikuntha will always be there. Radha knew this and so even when Krishna left and she wept, she never expected him to return physically; he was always with her emotionally. Uddhava still had to learn the lesson, to turn into a true goose, to enjoy the waters but not let the water stick to his feathers. Getting Uddhava to realize this truth, not merely understand it, is the best gift anyone could offer a friend.

Culture

13

River of rebirth

Chronicles known as Puranas narrate the tale of how Ganga came down to earth to help those who die take birth once more.

A king called Sagara was once performing a yagna. If the ritual was a success, he would become Indra, king of paradise, and have access to all the pleasures of the world, including immortality. But there was already an Indra in the sky, and he could not bear the idea of being replaced. So he stole Sagara's horse that was an integral part of the ritual and hid it in the hermitage of a sage called Kapil. The sons of Sagara looked everywhere for the horse. They dug so deep that they created a crater that eventually became the receptacle of the sea. Finally they found the horse in Kapil's hermitage and they accused Kapil of theft. Kapil's eyes were shut at this time, as he was lost in deep contemplation. He had no idea of Indra's mischief. Irritated by the disturbance, he opened his eyes. So fiery was his first glance that the sons of Sagara who stood before him shouting accusations burst into flames and were reduced to a heap of ash. Indra smiled and Kapil shut his eyes once again. A heartbroken Sagara wondered, 'My sons have been killed in their youth. I will die of old age. None of us will be Indra. The yagna had been abandoned midway. None of us will sip amrita, the nectar of immortality. None of us will experience unending joy. Is every living creature doomed to die, having lived such incomplete lives?' Sagara searched for an answer. So did his son Anshuman, and Anshuman's son Dilip, and finally Dilip's son Bhagirath. Bhagirath met Garuda, the eagle, the only creature who had defeated Indra in battle. He said, 'If the ashes of your ancestors are washed by the Ganga they will be reborn and have a second chance of life.' Unfortunately, the Ganga flowed in the sky. Bhagirath prayed to Brahma, father of all living creatures, and he promised to persuade the Ganga to descend on earth. 'But beware,' said the haughty river-goddess when compelled to descend, 'the force of my fall will surely wash away all life on earth and crush its very foundations.' Bhagirath therefore invoked Shiva. Shiva agreed to let the Ganga fall on his head and thus protect the earth from direct impact. The world watched the spectacle of water descending from the sky. Indra gloated, convinced that the Ganga would destroy all of humanity, and with that all threats to his reign. But when the Ganga fell on Shiva's head, she found his head was covered with thick matted hair, so thick and so densely matted that she found herself getting entangled and trapped. Far from washing away life and breaking the foundations of earth, the Ganga found herself locked up atop Shiva's head. She tried to find a way out, but Shiva's locks were like a labyrinth. There was no escape. She begged and cried and finally, Shiva relented and Ganga flowed out of Shiva's head, down the slopes of Kailasa, through the ravines of the Himalayas, on to the plains and finally towards the sea. Her bubbly movements irritated one sage called Jahnu who swallowed her whole, but when Bhagirath revealed the identity and importance of the river, he released the river through his ear, after which she came to be known as his daughter, Jahnavi.

The idea of rebirth and the Ganga cannot be separated. The river comes from the land of Indra, who has access to amrita, the nectar of immortality. Indra, the hero of Vedic hymns, lives the life everyone on earth wants to live. He is strong and powerful and attractive and invincible. All day he spends enjoying the good things in life. He does not fear ageing or death. Kings of the earth, such as Sagara, envy him. They all want to live Indra's perfect life. They spend their lifetimes working towards it. Eventually everyone fails— those who die young, like Sagara's sons, and even those who die old, like Sagara himself. And everyone wonders if there will ever be another chance to become Indra.

A dip in the Ganga is about getting a karmic clean slate, a chance to begin life with a new balance sheet. Throwing ashes in the Ganga is about giving the dead a chance to be reborn once more, hopefully in Indra's paradise, and enjoy all things that were denied in this life. Ganga thus is all about forgiveness and second chances. It is an idea that gives hope to humanity.

The doctrine of rebirth is perhaps informed by agricultural practices on the riverbank, where crops grow and are harvested every year with cyclical regularity. Every year there are the rains, the summer heat and the winter chill. Nothing lasts forever, but everything comes back eventually. But civilizations of Egypt, Mesopotamia and China were also nurtured on the banks of rivers. Rebirth never featured in their stories. All of them spoke of death and an endless afterlife. They built pyramids and tombs to the dead and kept the ashes of ancestors in urns and temples, to celebrate the life that was. They did not cremate the dead and scatter ashes in a river, in the hope of yet another life. This life was their one and only chance. In the river-valley civilizations of India, however, the idea of a second chance took root firmly, perhaps because of men like the Greek followers of Alexander the Great, identified as gymnosophists or the naked wise men, who imagined the world very differently.

The Ganga's story refers to several such naked wise men, such as Kapil and Jahnu and Gautama and Agastya, but none as spectacular and magnificent as Shiva, from whose dreadlocks springs the promise of rebirth in the form of the Ganga, and who smears his body with ash to remind all of the promise of soul that outlives death!

Shiva is the great destroyer whose worship scholars often fumble to explain. How can a destroyer be worshipped?

Few ponder over what Shiva actually destroys. Even today, writers on Shiva insist on describing him as 'destroyer of evil' or 'creative destroyer' which reveals this long discomfort with the term 'destroyer'. Yes, Shiva is the destroyer. He is Yamantaka, the destroyer of death, and Kamantaka, the destroyer of desire. He is the destroyer of limitations imposed by one life.

Shiva, and the gymnosophists who considered him Adinath, or the primal teacher, offer a dual promise: a temporal promise to live as many lives one wants trying to be Indra, and a transcendental promise to break free from this foolhardy quest someday. This is not redemption or salvation or liberation. This is not enlightenment. This is just the offer of infinite second chances. With this one offer, death ceases to be a full stop; it becomes a comma. Shiva, the destroyer of death, then becomes worthy of worship, as does the river sprouting from his head.

14

Seeing the invisible

The most fundamental Hindu ritual is the 'darshan'—gazing upon the image of the deity. You look at the deity and in most temples, the deity, with large silver eyes, gazes back at you.

The rishis were perhaps the first to do darshan, which is why they were called rishis, the ones who gazed. Rishis are seers. What did they see? Like everyone, they possessed drishti, the ability to see the visible and tangible, the sa-guna. But they also possessed divya-drishti, the ability to see the invisible and the intangible, the nir-guna. They could see what no one else could see. They could join the dots, create patterns, observe rhythms and this led to insight, hearing the inner voice that makes no sound but still can be heard. This was shruti, hearing of the soundless speech. This was Veda, wisdom, later transmitted through mantras or hymns and yantras or symbols.

All of us do darshan. But we are limited by drishti. We do not develop divya-drishti. Our gaze is limited by our prejudice. The media's gaze is influenced by the desire to be populist. The politician's gaze is shaped by the desire for power and votes. Civil society's gaze is limited by its assumption that wealth and power is obtained through exploitation. What we hear then is smriti, that which is remembered, that which is shaped by a reference point from our memory banks.

When we see a doctor who is skilled in his trade and cures many people, we assume he is 'God'—a wonderful, caring human being. When we later discover that he is a womanizer, we are angry with him, not with our assumptions.

When we see a cricketer who is magnificent at his game, we assume he is an honest man with integrity and use him in public service announcements that condemn corruption. Then we discover how he uses his popularity and brand equity to get tax benefits and change the real-estate rules to build his fancy apartment. We get disappointed with him, not with our imagination about him.

Most recently a popular yoga teacher was equated with a saint until he spoke of hurling stones against the establishment and displayed anything but mystical equanimity. Suddenly, our impression of him has changed, and we do not like what we see. We do not question why we saw what we saw.

Impressions are based on the visible. But beyond the visible is the invisible. When the invisible becomes visible, we are often shocked. We are shocked because we assume that what we see is infinite, when in fact the visible is always finite. When we meet an individual we have access only to that which is sa-guna about him or her. We judge people based on the sa-guna—what we see and what they show. We do not factor in the nir-guna—what we don't see and what they don't show. Even today we have in our minds 'good' people and 'bad' people. Judgements based on the sa-guna—are these judgements true? Are we setting ourselves up for future disappointments? This over-reliance on sa-guna is why our darshan does not reveal the Veda to us. We hear the prejudiced voice of smriti, not the insightful voice of shruti.

15

The song of the crow

Everyone wonders: Why do good things happen to bad people? Why do fortunes never come the way we desire? Why are we unhappy? Why do we have to marry and produce children? From these questions comes our understanding of the world.

The word 'why' is translated as 'ka' in Sanskrit, the sacred language of Hinduism. Ka is the first consonant of the Sanskrit alphabet. It is both an interrogation as well as an exclamation. It is also one of the earliest names given to God in Hinduism.

During funeral ceremonies, Hindus are encouraged to feed crows. The crow caws, 'Ka?! Ka?!' It is the voice of the ancestors who hope that the children they have left behind on earth spend adequate time on the most fundamental question of existence, 'Why?! Why?!'

In mythology there is a crow called Kakabhushandi who sits on the branch of Kalpataru, the wish-fulfilling tree. The tree fulfils every wish but is unable to answer Kakabhushandi's timeless and universal question, 'Ka?! Ka?!'

The question need not be 'why'. It can be 'who'. Who is responsible for giving me this life? Or it can be 'what'. What can be responsible for giving me this life? From the root 'ka' come the various interrogatives that are parts of Hindi, a modern Indian language which has Sanskrit as one of its major tributaries: what or kya, who or kaun, why or kyon, how or kaise.

The nineteenth-century European Orientalists presented Hinduism to the world as a religion when they discovered in Vedic scriptures an underlying thought that unified the diversity of Indian customs, hitherto deemed pagan and heathen. But the religions they were exposed to, such as Judaism, Christianity and Islam, tended to be prescriptive, with very clear rules and codes of conduct. Vedic is more reflective than prescriptive. Reflections are timeless and universal while prescriptions are contextual, specific to communities of a particular place in a particular period. Many therefore do not like viewing Hinduism as a religion and prefer to see it as a way of life. Reflections begin when we ask the question 'Why?' There is no hurry to conclude or to cling to a convenient answer. The exploration continues for as long as it takes, until one is satisfied.

In India, the answer offered for the circumstances over which one has no control is karma. Actions in our past lives determine the fortunes and misfortunes of this life. We thus are made responsible for our bodies and our families. Actions performed in this life will determine our body and our family in our next life.

Is this true? No one knows. But the consequences of believing it are far-reaching.

Belief in rebirth puts the responsibility of our life squarely on our shoulders. For actions that we committed we have been given the life that we are living. We may not remember those past actions, but we are responsible for the present moment, nevertheless.

Mandavya one day found himself being arrested and brutally punished by the king's guard for a crime he did not commit. 'Why?' he asked Yama, the god of death. Yama looked at the book of karma and replied, 'As a child you tortured insects. This is the reaction of that action. What seems unfair in one lifetime becomes fair when one considers several lifetimes.'

Who then is responsible for my life and my fortunes and misfortunes? I am. This means I cannot blame anyone for my misfortune—not my parents, not my circumstances, not my DNA, not even God.

Karma is loosely translated as fate.

Only humans can ask these questions and reflect on life. Ka? Because humans have an evolutionary advantage. We are blessed with the neo-frontal cortex, the part of the brain behind the forehead. This is the human brain located on top of the animal brain. It allows us to do what no other creature can do: it allows us to imagine!

Hindus smear their foreheads with ash or sandal paste or red kumkum powder. It is the dot known as bindi on the forehead of women. It is the vertical and upwardly directed line known as tilak on the forehead of men. It is a ritual through which voiceless ancestors are telling the children they left behind on earth: Use this unique organ behind your forehead. It is what makes you human!

Only humans can imagine a world that is distinct from reality. We can compare reality with an imagined reality and therefore wonder why reality is the way it is. We can imagine being born in another family and wonder: Why was I born in this one? We can imagine being born with a taller or shorter, fairer or darker body, and wonder: Why was I born with this one? Imagination propels us towards the question: Ka?

Imagination is translated as manas. Humans possess manas. Therefore, the human race is the race of Manavas, those who can imagine. The leader of the human race becomes Manu. Manas also means the mind, the mind which can take flight like a bird or slither like a serpent, and look at the world both broadly and narrowly, reflect on things here and not here, exist both here and now and also over there in the past and over here in the future.

While the human brain enjoys imagination, it does not enjoy introspection. Pondering on questions and seeking answers needs a lot of energy in the form of glucose. Glucose is a precious body fuel. The body would rather conserve this energy for moments of crisis. Naturally, though humans are the only creatures with the wherewithal to introspect, human physiology is geared to block this process. It takes a great amount of will to overpower this block and introspect and seek the answer to Ka. In a way, this is very similar to exercise. It demands huge will power. Few indulge in this quest. Fewer still are naturally inclined towards it. The one who indulges in this quest is called a brahmana.

The word brahmana is derived from the Sanskrit root 'brh', meaning 'to grow', and 'manas'. All living creatures grow physically after birth. But there is a limit to this physical growth. Humans are the only creatures capable of limitless growth. Why? Because of manas. The possibilities offered by imagination and introspection are infinite. The one who uses these infinite possibilities to discover Ka therefore becomes brahmana, the one with expanded imagination.

From the root 'brh' also comes the name of God. Not one, but two. One is Brahma. The other is brahmn. Notice the difference in spelling and the use of capitals. Brahma is pronounced by laying stress to the latter vowel; brahmn is pronounced laying stress on no vowel; brahmana is produced by laying stress to the first vowel and the last consonant. Brahma is a proper noun, brahmn is not considered a noun while brahmana is a common noun. Brahma is a finite personality, brahmn is an infinite abstract notion. The brahmana is the one who seeks to move from the finite to the infinite, from the form to the formless, from Brahma to brahmn.

Every human being is a Brahma. The day he seeks to decipher the puzzle of Ka, the song of the crow, he becomes a brahmana. Every human being has the wherewithal to realize

Ka, hence brahmn. Brahma is who we are while brahmn is who we can become. One transforms from Brahma to brahmn, from finiteness to infiniteness, from restlessness to repose, from anxiety to self-assurance, by using the neo-frontal contex to imagine and introspect. Bowing to deities in temples and fellow human beings is to remind those before us of the Vedic maxim, *Tat tvam asi,* meaning 'that's what you are'—you are Brahma who is capable of realizing brahmn. That's what I am too, hence *Aham Brahmasmi.*

16

Changing rituals

In the past ten years or so, wedding rituals have been changing across the country. This is most evident in the ritual called sangeet where families of the bride and groom, trained by professional choreographers, dance to Bollywood songs. This ritual has spread across communities, especially in cities and amongst the Indian diaspora. It has become a pan-Indian ritual: gaudy, secular and fun.

The ritual has its roots in north India and it has reached the world thanks to Bollywood which is dominated, and influenced, by north Indian film-makers (Johar, Kapoor, Chopra, Deol) and then the great teleserials that are being broadcast to every Indian home 24/7 by various television channels. Television has become the holy book of the twenty-first century, telling us how to live our lives.

Once, the sangeet was merely a very feminine ritual—

women of the bride's family came together to sing songs while bedecking the bride. It marked the transition of a young woman from virgin to wife. It was a rite of passage, one that helped the woman make her shift in consciousness. The songs were both bawdy and romantic—teasing the woman into sexual and emotional maturity that would be expected of her post-marriage.

Rituals play a key role in our lives. They give structure. They shape our days, our months, our years. They serve as milestones and help us go through life in an orderly way. Rituals make us believe that we are part of a plan, that life is not random, that all things have a meaning. Unlike stories that need to be heard and symbols that need to be seen, rituals are communications that need to be performed. Thus do they communicate.

Rituals can be individual rituals, family rituals or community rituals. Individual rituals are personal; they involve no other. Every individual has his very own ritual of bathing and eating and praying and sleeping. It defines who he or she is, and makes the follower feel disciplined and secure. Family rituals bind the family together. These are usually birth, death and marriage rituals. Finally, there are community rituals or festivals that bind society while marking the passage of time. They can be religious like Holi or secular like Independence Day. Both mark the passage of time. Holi marks the shift into summer. Independence Day marks the birth of one more year of freedom. Holi serves as a safety valve for the community psyche, as it allows public display of behaviour otherwise prohibited. Independence Day also has a psychological purpose—it reassures all Indians, as it reaffirms the idea of a nation state.

The Bollywoodized sangeet is a modern ritual for both the family and the community. It breaks free from the confines of religion, marks the transition of time and seems very logical and universal, as it offers no deep meaning other than fun. Yet, like all rituals, it has a deeply emotional and parochial purpose. Like all rituals, it subtly enforces a discourse. The value given to virginity in Catholicism manifests in the white gown and veil of the bride in church. The value given to fertility in Hinduism manifests in her red sari. The value given to unity is reinforced when all Indians are expected to stand during the national anthem. The same principle holds true for the Bollywoodized sangeet. By anchoring a momentous rite of passage of the bride to ideas emerging from a flaky film industry, we as a people are trying to construct (subconsciously, of course) for ourselves, as well as the rest of the world, that exasperatingly tenuous, politically correct, socially significant 'pan-Indian identity'.

17

Aspiration Nautanki

Kalidasa, the great Sanskrit poet, they say, was very market-savvy. On his way to the court of Vikramaditya, he would stop in villages and hamlets. He would be asked to perform and he would sing bawdy songs, similar to today's item numbers, to the delight of his audience. But in the king's court, he would sing the most polished verses with the most sophisticated vocabulary, figures of speech, metre, melody and metaphor. When asked why, he said, 'Nautanki is for the masses craving instant gratification. Natyashastra is for the patient aesthete, the connoisseur, the rasik; their numbers are very few.'

Nautanki responded to popular forces, Natyashastra aspired for perfection, not popularity. Nautanki spoke to the lowest common denominator and avoided making too much demand on the emotion or the intellect. Natyashastra sought the subtle, spoke to the soul and demanded a lot from the audience. Nautanki pleased the tired flesh after a day's work. Natyashastra sought to address the questions of the soul. Nautanki took us towards prakriti, connecting with our natural instincts. Natyashastra strove to take us towards sanskriti, towards the sophistication and nobility that humanity is capable of.

For centuries, both flourished. Each one had its place. Each one had its relevance. Nautanki thrived in bazaars and Natyashastra in temple compounds and royal courts and the courtyards of noblemen and courtesans. But in the twentieth century, the rise of communism led to attacks on the Natyashastra for being snobbish, arrogant, Brahmanical, pandering to upper-class hegemony. It became noble to focus on the masses, to democratize the arts. The twentieth century also saw the rise of capitalism, where market forces determined which art would survive. Considering its mass base, Nautanki would clearly win. So both ideology and economics have put Natyashastra on the back foot. The patronage is gone. And only the very determined survive.

So today, we have Bharatnatyam dancers dancing to Bollywood numbers and two-minute Kathakali performances. Yes, that really happens. If you criticize, you are reprimanded for stifling innovation, for being Brahmanical, for being a snob, for being out of touch with the youth and the masses.

At a party I attended recently the discussion revolved around the latest from Bollywood, 'I am your dog. You are my bitch.' Those who moaned at the collapse of decency and the rise of crass buffoonery in films were cornered with the lines, 'You may think it is stupid, but look at the money it made.' And you realize there is a new code in social circles: If you want to appear cool and democratic and with the masses, you must not display any displeasure at crass buffoonery, especially if it is a commercial success.

So imagine my horror when, while flipping through channels, I saw an anchor of a talk show, famous for her stylish pretentiousness, also submitting to crass buffoonery while conversing with a 'desirable' star. Nobody expects a talk show to be 'deep', but this 'shallow'? I mean, come on.

I refuse to make Nautanki aspirational. Not because Natyashastra is 'better' but because Natyashastra seeks to push the boundaries of human capability and capacity. It seeks to uplift, not merely to entertain. It demands faith and patience and rigour and there is absolutely no guarantee of critical or commercial success. It needs to be pursued for its own sake, like prayer. Like Kalidasa, some of us may have to pursue Nautanki on the side to pay the bills, or to stoke the ego with popularity. But validation and veneration of crass buffoonery—I draw the line there.

18

Dharma-sankat in family business

The oldest Indian epics, the Ramayana and the Mahabharata, revolve around family dramas.

The Ramayana tells the story of Rama of Ayodhya and his antagonist, Ravana, king of Lanka. The Mahabharata tells the story of Krishna and his warring cousins, the Pandavas and the Kauravas of Hastinapur. Another epic, the Bhagavata, often considered a prequel to the Mahabharata, tells the story of Krishna's early life in Gokul. Together these three epics deal with every possible family-related issue, from inter-generational conflict to succession planning to talent management to sibling rivalry. They are filled with thoughts and ideas that are considered timeless, hence of value even to modern family businesses as they go through dharma-sankat or ethical dilemmas in the new world order, where the demands of institutional business tower over traditional family assumptions.

1. What is a family?

Families in the Ramayana and the Mahabharata, significantly, are not defined by blood. Rama and Lakshmana are half-brothers, with a common father but different mothers. Of the five Pandava brothers, three have a common mother, and none have a common father. Krishna is raised by foster-parents, and even his brother Balabhadra is actually his half-brother. What defines a family then is not blood or law or custom, but trust. In a family governed by trust, there are no rules; only love defines all actions, as in the Bhagavata. In a family with no trust, rules have no role; only power defines all actions, as in the Mahabharata. In between stands the Ramayana, where there is love but also rules.

2. How critical are rules to bind a family together?

Rules are the fundamental building blocks of an institution. Members of an institution can be either the sheep who follows the rules or the independent goat who challenges the rules. Greek narratives understood the free-thinking goat. Biblical narratives celebrated the sheep and equated the goat with the Devil. In Indian epics, however, rules play second fiddle to intent. More important than compliance or defiance is the reason behind the compliance or the defiance.

Rama, hero of the Ramayana, keeps rules, and so does Duryodhana, villain of the Mahabharata. But Rama does it to ensure stability in Ayodhya while Duryodhana does it for his own satisfaction, and this results in the war at Kurukshetra. Krishna, hero of the Mahabharata, breaks rules but so does Ravana, villain of the Ramayana. Krishna does it to bring joy in Gokul with his many pranks as he goes about stealing butter, and with his ruthless war strategies to get justice for the Pandavas, while Ravana does it for his own satisfaction and causes the burning of his island kingdom of Lanka. Family businesses need Ramas and Krishnas who work for the welfare of the kingdom (symbol of business), not Ravanas and Duryodhanas who work for themselves.

3. What should be the relationship between family and the business?

In the Ramayana, the kingdom of Ayodhya is more important than Raghu-kula, the family that governs it. In the Mahabharata, the Kuru-kula family is more important than the kingdom of Hastinapur it is responsible for. In the Ramayana, Rama, son of King Dasharatha, upholds the tradition of the Raghu-kula, goes into exile so that the integrity of the royal family is never questioned and Ayodhya feels secure under its leadership. In the Mahabharata, Bhishma, son of King Shantanu, gives up conjugal life not for the sake of his kingdom, but so as to satisfy the lust of his father who wishes to marry Satyavati, the ambitious daughter of an ambitious fisherman. The kingdom of Ayodhya plays a key role in all decision making in the Ramayana. This is not so in the Mahabharata, which is why the kingdom of Hastinapur is divided and the kingdom of Indraprastha is gambled away.

But placing the institution over the family comes at a price in the Ramayana—the very same royal traditions (Raghu-kula-riti) that celebrate the obedience of the son also demand that a woman of tainted reputation should not be queen of Ayodhya. Thus Rama-rajya witnesses the rejection of Rama's innocent wife, Sita, whose abduction by Ravana makes her the subject of public gossip. It is a case of professional and personal conflict where profession wins. Rama's children grow up in the forest, not the palace. As the follower of the rules, Rama is not allowed to change the rules. But trust remains firm. Rama abandons the queen of Ayodhya but not his wife; he never remarries.

4. Does loyalty matter?

Loyalty to dharma matters more than loyalty to a person. Ravana has two brothers, Vibhishana and Kumbhakarna. The Ramayana celebrates Vibhishana who leaves Ravana's side and joins Rama, and berates Kumbhakarna who remains by Ravana's side till the very end. In the Mahabharata, the noble warrior, Karna, is killed for siding with the Kauravas and so is Shalya, king of Madra, who is tricked into fighting against the Pandavas.

Culture

Dharma is the journey of man out of animal instincts, where he outgrows his desire to be dominant and territorial. Both Ravana and Duryodhan are alpha males, lions that establish pecking orders, demand obedience and work for their own aggrandizement. They don't care for people. They use people as instruments. Both drag their brothers and sons to their death as they cling to their own desires. Such behaviour is acceptable in animals but not in humans. Rama and Krishna have outgrown the desire to dominate or establish territory. Thus, dharma is the journey from a Ravana mindset to a Rama mindset, from a Duryodhana mindset to a Krishna mindset. Dharma is about achieving a Vishnu mindset that ensures the flow of wealth into the kingdom.

Rama is a king who upholds the law not for personal ambition but because it is his duty. Krishna is a participant in a war not his own, to help transform five brothers from irresponsible gamblers to responsible rulers, even at the cost of his own family, who are cursed by the mother of the Kauravas following their final defeat.

5. What is the role of the leader?

Leader in Indian thought is called a Karta or a Yajaman. A Yajaman is not an alpha male who establishes pecking order and demands obedience. He increases the sensitivity of family members so that they take responsibility for themselves and the world that depends on the family. To do this, he has to increase his own sensitivity to the needs and wants of his own family. Thus, increased sensitivity towards responsibility in the family depends on the increased sensitivity of the Yajaman for the family. Their growth mirrors his growth.

6. Is the eldest the natural leader?

Rama is the eldest in his family but Krishna is not. With or without the crown, both act as leaders as they function as Yajaman, understanding people and enabling them to transform and grow.

Once Lakshmana, the loyal brother of Rama, complained to his brother, 'I always have to obey you because you are my elder brother.' Rama responded thus: 'In our next life, you will be the elder brother but you will still agree with me, not out of obligation or loyalty but because you will realize that all my actions are rooted in dharma.' And so Lakshmana was reborn as Balabhadra and Rama was reborn as his younger brother, Krishna. Krishna never obeyed Balabhadra but, after initial irritation, Balabhadra always understood.

7. How does one handle individual aspirations?

This is alluded to through the food and marital arrangements of the Pandavas.

When they were children, the mother of the Pandavas, Kunti, divided the food into two halves. One half was given to Bhima who had a great appetite. The second half was divided equally between the other four brothers and their mother. The brothers understood Bhima's need and there was no resentment.

When they got married, however, the brothers had to share their common wife equally. Each brother could spend only one year with her and then wait for four years before his next turn. Bhima did not resent this. And when Arjuna accidentally interrupted Yudhishthira when he was with Draupadi, he accepted his punishment of a year's exile with grace.

In the household of Draupadi, no one husband was dominant, even though Yudhishthira was the official Yajaman. To satisfy his individual aspiration, each Pandava brother was allowed to have another wife. But this second wife was not allowed to live in the same household as Draupadi. It was a separate house where the brother could also be Yajaman.

8. Why do break-ups happen?

Break-ups happen when the Yajaman fails, trust collapses and territoriality rises. Basically, when trust and dharma give way to the insecure animal within.

In the Ramayana, stability of the family and kingdom is not the result of Rama being eldest or talented, or because of his brothers' loyalty, but because every brother displays integrity and sensitivity in the face of crisis. Technically, Rama's other brother, Bharata, could have taken over the kingdom after his mother had secured two boons from the king: exile of Rama and coronation of Bharata. But he refuses. To accept would be turning into a Duryodhana, focusing on the letter of the law, not the spirit. He refuses to be an opportunist alpha male. For he knows that that will be the collapse of the family order and inspire other brothers to follow suit. Bharata and Rama are thus both Yajamans, understanding their responsibility to each other, the family and Ayodhya.

In the Mahabharata, like Rama, Bhishma gives up his claim to the throne for the benefit of his half-brothers. His half-brothers however do not behave like Bharata. They claim the throne. Things go downhill after that, as no one behaves like a Yajaman. Bhishma's eldest grand-nephew, Dhritarashtra, is not allowed to be king because he is blind, resulting in a lifelong resentment in his children, the Kauravas; the second grandchild, Pandu, is allowed to be king but he is unable to father children and so needs the help of the gods to create the five Pandavas. Focus of the cousins is all about inheritance rights, not royal responsibilities. Dharma collapses. Rather than share, the kingdom ends up being divided. But even that does not solve the problem. No one has transformed. The Kauravas remain resentful, spiteful, insecure and jealous. Krishna intervenes, as there is no Yajaman around. He hopes to inspire the next generation of kings to rise above their animal nature and in doing so enable others around them to rise above animal nature. The process is not easy. It demands many a sacrifice, years of exile, humiliation, war and bloodshed.

9. How must talent be nurtured?

The ashrama system of Vedic times was an attempt to ensure a smooth transition to the next generation of kings while the old king was alive. After being a student, one became a Yajaman or head of the household. Then when the son came of age, one had to retire and finally renounce the world.

Retirement was a critical step, a quarter of one's lifetime, when one stepped away from actively running the business to enabling the future generation to take over the reins. The point was to render oneself useless over a period of time so that when it was time to renounce the world, the next generation was already running the show responsibly. Thus, a vast proportion of time was invested in the next generation.

This explains Dasharatha's decision to retire when Rama comes home with a wife. Bhishma, however, is never happy with the capabilities of the next generation and refuses to retire even after his grand-nephews (the Pandavas and the Kauravas) have children of their own. His overprotective nature results in overdependence upon him. No talent is nurtured and the family collapses. In the end, Bhishma has to be pinned to the ground with arrows, so that a new world order can finally be established.

10. What about daughters taking over family businesses?

Mythology is symbolic. It must not be taken literally.

Ideas are communicated through male and female forms. For example, a male form represents king while a female form represents kingdom, thus indicating the mutual dependence. Without either there is neither. Somewhere along the way, there was confusion between the idea and the form (vehicle of the idea). Rather than representing kingship, men became identified with kings, while women, rather than representing kingdom, became identified as kingdom, hence property.

Stripped of patriarchal bias and literal analogies, Rama, Krishna, Ravana and Duryodhana are mindsets that can exist in men or women. Vishnu is the mindset that ensures prosperity, hence Lakshmi. Anyone can be Vishnu, a daughter as much as a son.

11. How does one cope with a shift in values over generations?

Rama upholds dharma very differently from Krishna. One upholds the rule while the other breaks it. This is because the two belong to very different yugas, or contexts. Rama belongs to Treta Yuga and Krishna to Dvapara Yuga. The conditions of the world in each Yuga is different and so is the response to it. Awareness of this change is critical.

In an earlier age, the Krita Yuga, when kings of the earth broke all rules, Vishnu descended as Parashurama. He killed all kings. But then he saw a king called Rama. Impressed by Rama's nobility, Parashurama withdrew from the world. Ability to change with yugas is the hallmark of Vishnu. To cope with the shift in values over generations, Yajmans have to strive to be Vishnu.

12. How can professionals be included in family businesses?

India is named Bharata-varsha after a king called Bharata (son of Shakuntala, not to be confused with Rama's brother). The story goes that his wives gave him many sons but he rejected them all as they did not 'look' like him. So he invoked the gods and the gods gave him Vithata, an illegitimate, abandoned child. Vithata ended up being Bharata's heir. This indicates the value Bharata gave to the kingdom he was responsible for. His sons did not match up to his expectations and so he considered an outsider. This is not an easy task and perhaps because Bharata succeeded in taking such a monumental decision, the entire subcontinent came to be named after him.

Often the Yajaman has to struggle between family members and professionals. Family members are viewed as 'mine' and professionals are viewed as 'not mine'. With the former there is more trust while with the latter there is more transaction. Because family members are mine, there is room for more assumptions, more allowances and more risks, which is not possible with professionals. The professionals, because they are expected to be professional, are encouraged not to have emotional attachment to the business and focus only on the rules. They are expected to be more logical and less emotional, hence less prejudiced, which an enterprise needs. Unfortunately, what is 'mine' for the Yajaman ends up becoming 'not mine' for the professional. This creates a distance that is difficult to bridge. Often the professional thinks he is Rama, but the family looks at him as Duryodhana. Or the professional believes he is Krishna, but the family is convinced he is Ravana. Sometimes, the Yajaman thinks of the professional as Rama and Krishna, making the family insecure, and its members refusing to see the professional in the same light.

In the Ramayana, Rama does not consider Ayodhya 'mine'. He does not derive his identity from it. Hence he is able to give it up with ease. Ayodhya is not his territory that secures his self-image. Unfortunately, for most entrepreneurs, businesses are territories that secure their self-image and the self-image of their family. Detachment is not easy.

Governance rules will never create a Rama. And Rama does not need governance rules to decide who will bring greater value to Ayodhya: a son, a daughter, a nephew, a niece or a professional.

19

Mara, D. K. Bose

There are two stories of word reversal: one comes from mythology, another comes from Bollywood. Both deal with rage and helplessness.

This one is from mythology. Poverty forced Ratnakara to become a highway robber. He justified his actions on the grounds that he had to feed his family. 'Will your family share the burden of your crimes?' he was once asked. When he checked, his family said, 'No!' It was his responsibility to feed them, they said, and they did not really care how he did it, by fair means or foul. Ratnakara felt betrayed and lost. 'How do I unburden my soul?' He was told to chant the one word that bothered him the most. So Ratnakara chanted the word 'Mara'. 'Mara, Mara, Ma-Ra, Ma-Ra, Ma, Ra, Ma, Ra-Ma, Ra-Ma, Rama, Rama, Rama, Rama, Rama!' As the word got reversed so did his mind, from rage and anger and helplessness to hope and peace and forgiveness. For 'Mara' means death and desolation. In Buddhism, it means the demon of desire who fetters us in the world of unhappiness. From Mara comes the word 'maru' meaning desert. Rama is the opposite of all this—life, immortality, liberation, joy, God!

This one is from Bollywood. A son feels shame and guilt, as he does not match up to his father's expectations. His father says what he expected to be a bar of soap turned out to be nothing but empty, gassy foam. He will not commit suicide: he has seen well-timed posters of an earnest-looking actor telling him to focus on his needs and not be overrun by parental ambition. Spiritual gurus are no help; they are busy playing politics. So all he can do is sing, using the template inherited by hard rockers, angry face, angry tunes and a guitar. The wannabe wants to say F*** and C***, which like most swear words used by angry men, refer to female sexuality disparagingly. But he can't. The audience prefers equally foul Hindi swear words. But even that he cannot say. The censor board will not allow him. So he comes up with a poetic device. Just keep repeating in the song the name of 'D. K. Bose'. When repeated again and again and again it will reverse to give you a juicy swear word. How cool is that! An adult film with some clever titillation is necessary to satisfy the teenage audience.

In the former story, the word is twisted to help a man transcend his rage and helplessness. In the latter story, the word is twisted to vent youth angst. Twisting in the first case is necessary, as it is the only word which clouds the robber's mind. His tongue is too sullied to make room for the name of God. Twisting in the second case becomes necessary, as civil society will not allow the vocabulary of society's underbelly to surface. What follows is the Bollywood song twisting and bending and manipulating the rules of the game, a cleverness displayed by film-makers, a cleverness that is mostly used by politicians, a cleverness that is, unfortunately, also the root of all corruption. Civil society does not approve but can do nothing about it, except watch in silent dismay. At the most, it can fast!

We condemn such cleverness as it makes censor boards and all laws quite stupid. But sometimes we need a safety valve, as in a pressure cooker, to express our venomous rage. That is why in temple rituals there is something called 'ninda-stuti' which involves abusing the resident deity, once popular in traditional society but now shunned, even denied, by modern sanitized religion. This ritual allows the devotee to shout and scream at God, say things worse than 'Mara' and 'D. K. Bose', until he finds peace.

20

Babbling in India

Have you noticed that telemarketers are now talking to you in Hindi or Marathi? That is the first assumption, and only later do they switch to English. Have you noticed that when you call a bank or a mobile company, you are asked to choose a preferred language? English is not the only choice, and often not the first choice.

The fact is that less than 20 per cent of India speaks in English; the rest speak some regional language. Until recent times, the rest of India mattered only to the government and politicians, not to the corporate world. Now, as markets in Europe and America are shrinking and the West is moving in to harvest Indian markets, suddenly the 80 per cent non-English-speaking mass of India has started to matter, for everything from loans to cell phones.

Language is power. In ancient India, Sanskrit was spoken

by the elite, the rest spoke Prakrit. Ancient dramatists gave Sanskrit dialogues to the kings but Prakrit dialogues to servants and women. The word Prakrit comes from 'prakriti', or nature, suggesting that Prakrit is a more organic language rooted to the earth. Sanskrit, a highly polished and highly structured language, was believed to be the language of the gods in the safekeeping of priests and kings.

English is the new Sanskrit. If you are elite, you speak English; the rest speak other Indian languages. So if you want to show that you are moving up in life, you make sure you speak English. But if you want votes or market share, you speak in a regional language. To reach out to the masses, you abandon English and speak in Hindi or Marathi or Telugu or Tamil or Bengali. Language is no longer just a means to communicate; it is a way to acquire power. Even MTV surrendered to Hindi so that it reaches small-town India.

In the Bible, we are told that initially all humans spoke the same language. They came together to build a tower that would reach up to the heavens. This Tower of Babel was built as an expression of self-aggrandizement. To humble them, God twisted tongues and got everyone to speak a different language. Different languages resulted in the creation of different nations scattered across the world. Different nations meant conflicts, infighting and disunity.

The desire to unite people with a single language has its benefits. Most north Indians, for example, do not know that there is a Ramayana in almost every Indian language. There may be the *Tulsi Ramayana* in Hindi but there is the *Kamban Ramayana* in Tamil and the *Toda Ramayana* in Telugu and the *Krittivasa Ramayana* in Bengali and the *Bhavarta Ramayana* in Marathi and the *Giridhar Ramayana* in Gujarati. Not only is the language different but with different languages come different nuances, unique to that language.

In the Valmiki Ramayana, for example, there is no Lakshmana-rekha. This idea came from regional Ramayanas. English translators of the Mahabharata were so embarrassed by the explicit sexual descriptions in Sanskrit that some verses were translated in Latin. Our understanding of culture will always be restricted by the number of languages we know.

21

Not sparing the Gita

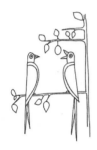Now that Rama and the Ramayana are not yielding political dividends, it is the time of Krishna and the Gita to be exploited in the political arena. So now a government wants to impose the 'song of God' on all students. And television channels are drawing attention as to how 'minorities' are upset.

What about 'majorities'? Are they happy about it? Encouraged by the media, we assume that the right-wing is the voice of the majority. The media implicitly imposes the idea that right-wing politicians are the voice of religion. This is done to create good narratives. Good narratives are based on conflicts. Conflicts give us good ratings and sales. What better way to create conflict than to get two right-wing guys with opposing ideologies into the ring? Better still, a right-wing hooligan and a left-wing intellectual. And so the story that is told on television and newspapers is driven by the result that is desired—the very thing the Gita warns us against.

At a recent conference, I presented my ideas on values. My presentation, as usual, contained calendar art of Hindu gods and goddesses. A well-meaning journalist pounced on me and kept pounding me, to the amusement of the audience. While the audience understood the message, the journalist clearly focused on the medium: Hindu deities! She saw red.

Like the Pavlovian response of a dog who salivates when a bell rings because long ago the bell was accompanied by food, she imagined me as a saffron-robed right-wing politician and kept pounding me and felt good about it. It was not a pleasant experience but there was nothing I could do. If I argued or explained, it would only reinforce her view that I was against 'minorities'. She was the saviour, the martyr, the prophet, leading India to the Promised Land. She had imagined me as the brutal pharaoh who enslaves India with religious ideas. I was the nail and she was the self-righteous hammer, gleefully pounding me.

Of course, when I used Biblical metaphors, she was a bit lost. How could this 'Hindu' be so comfortable and reverential about a Biblical narrative? This did not fit into her world view. 'People need to be led,' she yelled. And I realized she imagined herself, as a journalist, to be a noble shepherd tending to the sheep of India, while she imagined all politicians as wolves. I saw the wolf within her, but there was no use pointing it out. She would bite my head off.

It is this imagination that is getting out of hand. The imposition of the Gita, like the fight over Rama in the recent past, has nothing to do with Hinduism and everything to do with politics. But few point this out. The media focuses on the annoyance of 'minorities' but never the exasperation of the 'majorities'. Implicitly, majorities are evil and one needs to be wary of them.

Hinduism has no single leader. In fact, the same holds true for other religions. Both Christianity and Islam have many denominations. As does Judaism and Buddhism. But the media goes after the foulest fundamentalist in religious garb and cleverly presents them as the voice of the religion. It helps that these self-appointed guardians of the faith are attention-seeking providers of volatile soundbites. Who can beat reality-show-style video slaughter, I say?

Actions driven by an eye for the results lead to bloodbath and sorrow, says Krishna to Arjuna. Politicians are doing it. Journalists are doing it. Fundamentalists are doing it. For the next few days, everyone will fight over the Gita. Everybody will read the news. But few will actually read the book.

22

Outsourcing the storytelling grandmom

What is the difference between one culture and another? Every culture looks at the world differently and so has different notions of righteousness and propriety and aesthetics (what in India is called Satyam, Shivam and Sundaram). These are transmitted very overtly through stories and less overtly through symbols and rituals. The onus of transmitting them has been with the grandmother. Or at least that is what we assume.

But things have changed in the twentieth century. Suddenly, the grandmother can be outsourced—to books and radio and cinema and television and the Internet. A hundred years ago, few had access to books and fewer still could read. But today, stories are everywhere—even in newspapers and advertisements, shaping our notions of Satyam, Shivam and Sundaram. So who transmits values to our children today? How? And more importantly, what are the values we want to transmit?

Today's grandmother would have been born in post-Independence India, in all probability. She would be around sixty years old today. She would have been raised in a land that celebrated socialism, frugality and Gandhian simplicity. In her youth, as she raised her children, she would have experienced the horrific Emergency, the shattering of the post-Independence dream, the hollow cries to remove poverty, the draconian licence raj that spawned smugglers of the Bollywood screen. She would have envied her cousins who had moved to England and America for a better life. Her children would have been told to study hard so that they could get good jobs either in the government or as accountants, engineers and doctors, or better still, emigrate. And then the liberalization would have come; suddenly, wealth, the Internet and mobile phones would appear everywhere. Her children don't have to leave India to live a comfortable life. It is possible here in India and now she is the object of her cousins' envy.

Today she sits at home, watches television soap operas, reads scam-drenched newspapers and pulp novels, and condescends (because now it is a choice not an obligation, just like the daughter-in-law's career) to take care of the grandchildren or at least watch over the maid hired to take care of them, while her children are hard at work. She would now be part of her children's double-income, one-kid family, unlike the single income, two-kid family she raised. What stories will she tell her grandchildren? What values will she instil in them?

Will she tell them simplicity and discipline are good, influenced by the socialism era? Or will she tell them that wealth and indulgence are good, influenced by the liberalization era? Will her good-old-days be the stories of Balraj Sahani, the upright farmer of the 1950s; or of Amitabh Bachchan of the '70s, the angry young man; or the stories of Shah Rukh Khan of the '90s, who is rich and brash and romantic? Each story will present a different value system and none will prepare the child for the future that is as yet unknown. What if she chooses to outsource storytelling to television? What if 'traditional' Indian values end up with what the twenty-first-century Ekta Kapoor serials were all about—gaudy rituals without meaning, masking dark human manipulations?

People often mistake values for prescriptions. 'Honesty is the best policy' is not a value; it is a prescription. Everybody lies sometimes, depending on the context. Values are about figuring out why honesty is important and why sometimes we succumb to dishonesty. Values are not a set of rules or regulations, they are not a code of conduct; they are the reason why that rule or regulation or code of conduct exists. Often the grandmother cannot articulate it. It has been articulated by the story that the culture considers sacred. Thus, narration of 'sacred' stories is critical for value transmission and not stories per se, a fact that is often forgotten.

Stories are of two types—one set of stories is limited by history and geography, while another set has no such limitations. Ancient Indian sages called the former smriti, born of human memory, and the latter shruti, that which was heard (by meditating and reflective sages). The former contains values that are subject to the events and impressions of that period. The latter contains values that are believed to have come from a source that is non-human, hence timeless and universal; these tend to be classified as religious.

A non-religious story may seem non-religious, but they are rooted in religious values. The notion of rebirth will be distinctly absent in cultures that believe in one life. That the Jatakas speak of the past life of the Buddha means that Buddhism values rebirth. That European fairy tales always speak of 'happily ever after' means that Europe was influenced by the notion of Heaven found in the Bible.

A grandmother has a choice. She can tell stories influenced by her own memories, by history taught in schools, by stories she has read in novels or seen in Bollywood or teleserials. Or she can tell stories that have always been told as part of culture. The mythological narratives—the story of Shiva and Rama and Krishna and Durga. Or narratives from the Bible or the Koran or the Jatakas.

Then comes the political problem. Are these not religious stories? Can culture be separated from religion? Can there be Indian values separate from Hindu or Sikh or Muslim values? Are there human values? The ugly truth is—there are no universal values.

Values are a human construction, not a natural phenomenon. In nature, there are no values. What matters is survival at any cost. The idea of values is a product of human imagination. We imagine a world where might is not right, where even the meek have rights. From this imagination come values, hence culture. And because different people around the world have different imaginations, there are different values and hence different cultures.

When people seek storytelling grandmoms who will pass on values, what people are actually seeking are not 'values' but 'identity'. We fear our children are looking at the world very differently. They are imagining life very differently. We fear they are drifting into another subjective reality constructed by the media and Facebook and Twitter and Cartoon Network. We feel helpless before such massive forces. Identity is not natural, it is cultural; and cultures change over space and time. We want it to be fixed. But we fail because values change over time. What was okay then may not be okay today. Thus the storytelling grandmom has to keep reinventing herself, from generation to generation, and hope that the values she passes on to the grandchildren will sustain them through at least one more generation.

23

Peace with three worlds

Every Hindu ritual ends with three words, 'Shanti, Shanti, Shanti-hi,' which is conventionally translated as 'Let there be peace, peace, peace.' Why is the word repeated three times? And can there truly be peace in the world?

To assume that a world of peace can ever exist is considered naïve in Hinduism. To survive, every creature needs food. To get food, animals have to turn into predators and kill. Violence plays a key role in supporting life. As long as there is need for food, there will be predation, hence violence, hence no peace. Humans kill more than other living creatures because we hoard more food than we need to live, to insure ourselves against future scarcity. Every field, orchard, garden that provides us with food is established by destroying an ecosystem. Raw materials for industry can only be provided by destroying ecosystems. Human society is thus built on violence. Hinduism acknowledges this truism, which is why Hindu gods bear weapons in their hands. With such a pragmatic approach to violence, why do Hindu rituals repeat this chant for peace? And why three times?

In Shiva temples, the bilva sprig is offered to Shiva. The sprig has three leaves. Shiva's sacred mark comprises three horizontal lines. Shiva holds a trident which has three spikes. Shiva has three eyes—the left, the right and the central. He is called Tripurantaka—destroyer of three cities. Perhaps the secret of the chant for triple peace rests here.

Shiva is the archer who struck down three cities with a single arrow. The bow is the symbol of balance. To shoot it, one needs focus. To shoot three cities with a single arrow, one needs to be patient and aware until the three cities are perfectly aligned. All these characteristics suggest that Shiva's archery is a metaphor for yoga. Yoga makes the mind quiet, so that we are aware, patient, balanced and focused. In this state, we discover the three cities that we inhabit.

The three cities are: our body, all things over which we claim ownership and all things over which we do not claim ownership. In other words, 'me, mine and not-mine'. Ownership is human delusion—humans believe they have legitimate rights over the earth and hence have the notion of property that we can possess, buy, sell and bequeath to the next generation. Property is a cultural concept, not a natural concept. This is humanity's great delusion.

Yoga helps us realize that we own nothing in his world. We are born without possessions and we die without possessions.

Realizing this, we destroy 'mine and not mine'. Yoga also helps us realize that 'me' is not the body. We have a false identity, aham, the ego, that depends on the body and will die, and a true identity called atma, the soul, that does not depend on the body and will never die. True wisdom makes itself accessible when we outgrow our dependence on 'me, mine and not-mine'.

So the chant, 'Shanti, Shanti, Shanti-hi', does not mean, 'Let there be peace, peace, peace'. It means, 'Let me come to terms with the limitations of me, mine and not-mine'. It is the ultimate goal of Hinduism: to outgrow aham and realize atma.

24

Rules do not make Rama

 *If there were no rules, would we be corrupt? Do rules make us corrupt? After all, only when there are rules can rules be broken or bent. Only when there are rules do we have need for regulators and courts and auditors to keep watch over society. What would the world be without rules? The world without rules is the jungle – where might is right and only the fit survive. Humans made rules so that the meek can also inherit the earth, so that even the unfit can thrive. That is why rules exist. That is how human society came into being.*

Both the Ramayana and the Mahabharata are about human society and about rules. In the Ramayana, Rama follows the rules but in the Mahabharata, Krishna breaks the rules. We are told that both are righteous. Both uphold dharma. Both are forms of God. Both fight corruption. How can that be?

In the Ramayana, the villain breaks rules. Neither Surpanakha nor Ravana respect the laws of marriage. Surpanakha uses force to get rid of competition and get herself a desirable mate. Ravana uses cunning to steal another man's only wife, despite having many of his own. In contrast, in the Mahabharata, the villain does not break a single rule. No one—neither Bhishma nor Drona nor Karna nor the Pandavas—cries foul when a woman is dragged and disrobed in public, as technically, Duryodhana has not broken a single rule in the gambling hall. A rule-following Rama can combat a rule-breaking Ravana. But would he succeed against a rule-following villain like Duryodhana? That is why even God had to change his avatar and become Krishna, who bends the laws of nature and gets cloth to materialize to rescue Draupadi from her shame.

Corruption is not about breaking the rules: corruption is about rejecting our human side, embracing our animal side and reserving resources for the mighty and dominating the meek. Corruption is about becoming the territorial alpha male who excludes competition and includes no one, except those who surrender to him.

In India, every politician follows the rules, and every bureaucrat follows the rules, and every judge follows the rules. There are many rules to follow! Despite this, land is grabbed but no one is arrested or punished. Riots take place, hundreds are killed, but despite inquiry commissions, no one is convicted. Rapes take place but rapists are released on technicalities. There are never enough witnesses and not enough evidence. Even a terrorist who murders people in front of rolling cameras remains an 'alleged' criminal, and perhaps a political pawn, for months and years.

So the rage of the common man is understandable. So the outrage when Anna is put in jail is understandable. The government seems to be full of Bhishmas and Dronas and Karnas and the Pandavas—all rules are being followed while India is being disrobed. Expression of outrage gets you to Tihar Jail.

Within Tihar Jail, you find criminals: 'alleged' criminals as far as the court is concerned. These are high-profile politicians who have broken the law; small fish who everyone knows will in time be honourably discharged because there will not be any evidence and not enough witnesses and because our complex laws can be read in myriad ways by brilliant lawyers.

In this scenario, the Lokpal Bill is yet another set of laws and rules and auditors hoping to cleanse the country. Will it really stop the Ravanas? Or will it create many smarter Duryodhanas? Will it create more Ramas or will it hinder the Krishnas?

The point is not about the absence of suitable laws; it is about the absence of integrity. Let us not forget, we have the best Constitution in the world. This has been changed over eighty times in sixty years! What does it say about us?

Every person who follows the rule imagines himself to be a Rama, but his enemies see him as a Duryodhana. Everybody who breaks the rules imagines himself to be a Krishna, but his enemies see him as a Ravana. For the government, Team Anna is a rule-breaker while for Team Anna, the government is the rule-breaker. Team Anna imagines itself as a rule-keeper and so does the government. Who is being objective, I wonder?

The courts can only tell us if rules are broken or not broken. But the question today is about intent. Intent is invisible, intangible and subjective. Yes, as humans we may have moved out of the jungle but clearly the jungle has not moved out of humans. That is why our streets and jails and governments are full of stubborn alpha males, each one smug and self-righteous and highly territorial, wanting to dominate the other. Stripped and abused, India weeps in the gambling hall, while her adults point fingers at each other like children in a playground.

25

The offering of hair

So there is a photograph of our former cricket captain M. S. Dhoni with his head shaved. The hair has been offered to the gods. So here is the youth icon admitting that it is not all about skill or talent or leadership; it is also about divine grace. And for that you have to be grateful.

In the five years before 2011, one has observed M. S. Dhoni's hair change from long and streaked to neat and short, to fully shaved! And in many ways it reflects the growing up of a boy from a raging leonine individualist to a responsible team player, to a sensitive leader.

Hair is a powerful metaphor in Hindu mythology. A lot has been said about hair. Krishna has curly hair. Balarama has straight, silky hair. Shiva has thick, matted hair. The goddesses—Lakshmi, Saraswati and Durga—have loose, unbound hair. Hair has long been used in India to convey a message.

Unbound, unruly hair represents wild nature. Well-oiled and combed hair represents culture. That is why the wild Kali's hair is unbound while the domestic Gauri's hair is well bound and in her temples devotees make offerings of gajra, a string of flowers to tie up the hair. In the Mahabharata, Draupadi's unbound hair represents her fury. In the Ramayana, the last jewel of Sita is the hairpin that she gives Hanuman to convey to Rama that her honour, and his reputation, stand in a precarious position. Shiva's dreadlocks represent the potent power of his mind that enables him to catch and bind the unruly and wild river goddess, Ganga.

Shaving the head is associated with asceticism. Buddhist monks shaved their heads. Jain monks plucked their hair from the roots; to survive the pain is to convey that one is willing to suffer the challenges offered by monasticism. Brahmins shaved their heads but left a tuft in the end, an indicator that they were not monks but very much part of worldly life. This Brahmin tuft is tied up to show control; Chanakya of legend famously untied this tuft to display his rage and tied it only when the Nanda dynasty of Magadha had been brought to its knees. The hair of widows was shaved to enforce monasticism on them. It was this or the pyre, in medieval India, for those unfortunate women. The head is shaved to display bereavement as well as devotion, as in the case of Dhoni.

It is the Roman army that introduced the crew cut to this world. Before that men had long beautiful hair that the enemy could hold to pull you back and cut your throat in the battlefield. It is the Romans who associated the long hair of man with barbarians.

In orthodox Judaism, Christianity and Islam, hair is associated with sensuality and so is covered, especially when one is praying. This applies for both men and women which is why the cap is worn by orthodox Jewish and Muslim men at the time of prayer, a practice observed even by Sikhs, whose women cover their heads with a veil. To display hair is to display vanity. And modern men and women are okay with it. And so men and women colour their hair and allow it to grow, to make individualistic statements—until they want to be leaders and want to be taken seriously.

Culture

26

Mahabharata inside the house

When a family business breaks down, one is reminded of an old Indian tradition: never read the Mahabharata inside the house, always the Ramayana. For the Mahabharata is the tale of a household divided while the latter is the story of a household united.

The Ramayana speaks of three sets of brothers: those of Rama, those of Sugriva and those of Ravana. An exploration of the relationship of these three sets of brothers throws light on that one principle which can make or break a household, or indeed any organization.

Rama is asked to give up his claim to the throne and go into the forest so that his younger brother, Bharata, can be king in his stead. Rama does so without remorse or regret. Bharata, however, refuses to take a kingdom obtained through his mother's guile. He chooses to serve as regent until Rama's return. Another brother, Lakshmana, follows Rama into the forest to share his suffering and give him company.

Sugriva is driven out of his kingdom, Kishkindha, by his own brother, Vali. The two brothers were supposed to share their father's throne but following a misunderstanding, Vali is convinced that his brother wants the kingdom all for himself and in fury drives away Sugriva, ruling out all possibilities of reconciliation.

Ravana too drives out his brother, Kubera, to become king of Lanka. But neither has he any inheritance rights over Lanka nor is there any misunderstanding between him and Kubera. His is an action purely motivated by sibling rivalry. When Ravana abducts Rama's wife, Sita, one of his brothers, Vibhishana, turns away from him on moral grounds but another brother, Kumbhakarna, stays loyal to him.

The epic asks: Who is the good brother? Is it the selfless Rama, the upright Bharata or the obedient Lakshmana? Who is the bad brother – Sugriva who uses Rama to kill Vali? The ambitious Ravana, the traitor Vibhishana or the loyal Kumbhakarna? The answer is not simple as it first appears.

Rama gives up his claim to the throne not out of brotherly love but because dharma demands he respect his father's wish that he give up his claim to the throne. Bharata returns Ayodhya not out of love for Rama but because dharma frowns upon trickery. Yes, Lakshmana follows Rama out of filial love but later in the epic Rama teaches him a tough lesson.

One day, Rama asks Lakshmana not to let anyone enter

his chambers as he is giving a private audience to Kala, the god of time. Lakshmana obeys, saying, 'I shall kill whoever tries to disturb you.' No sooner is the door shut than Rishi Durvasa, renowned for his temper, demands a meeting with Rama. Lakshmana tries to explain the situation. 'I don't care,' says an impatient and enraged Durvasa. 'If I don't see the king of Ayodhya this very minute I shall curse his kingdom with drought and misfortune.'

At that moment Lakshmana wonders what matters more: his love for his brother which manifests as obedience or a royal family's duty to protect their kingdom? He concludes that Ayodhya is more important and so opens the door to announce Durvasa, interrupting Rama's meeting, an act for which he has to, to be true to his own enthusiastic declaration, kill himself. Inside, Lakshmana finds Rama alone. No sign of Kala. Outside there is no Durvasa. Lakshmana realizes this was Rama's way of saying that dharma matters more than filial love or obedience.

But what is dharma? It is often translated to mean duty or righteous conduct. But at a fundamental level, dharma is what distinguishes man from animals; it is what makes man human. All other living creatures subscribe to matsya nyaya or law of the jungle: might is right. But man is capable of reversing the law. In human society, might need not be right. The weak can have rights too. Even the feeble can thrive. An ideal human society is one based not on power and domination as in nature, but on the very opposite—love and generosity.

Vali does not display this love and generosity when he is eager to believe the worst about Sugriva. Rama does not tolerate this. When Rama kills Vali, Vali says, 'I could have saved Sita from you because I am stronger than Ravana.' To this, Rama replies, 'I killed you not to gain an ally in Sugriva but to establish the law of Bharata.' Bharata here refers to Rama's brother, temporary regent of Ayodhya and 'law of Bharata' means dharma, the code of civilization, that Rama's family has subscribed to for generations.

Vali then accuses Rama of killing him unfairly while he was engaged in a duel with Sugriva. In response, Rama says, 'Fighting for the dominant position is the way of animals. Those who choose to live by the law of the jungle must allow themselves to be killed by the law of the jungle, which makes no room for fair play. By destroying you I will, through Sugriva, institute the law of Bharata in this land so that henceforth the mighty do not dominate the meek.'

Ravana, though highly educated, also does not subscribe to dharma when he drives his own brother out of Lanka and claims his throne. This behaviour of domination and force, suitable for animals but unsuitable for humans, is repeated when he abducts Rama's wife, Sita. Loyalty to Ravana is not about loyalty—it is about rejection of dharma. That is why Rama kills Kumbhakarna and makes Vibhishana king of Lanka.

The Ramayana is an epic about what humans can be. By destroying Vali and Ravana, Rama destroys the animal instinct of domination. That is why Vali is called a monkey and Ravana a demon while Rama is purushottama, the perfection of man. The epic never makes a virtue of brotherly love or loyalty. It transcends such myopic views on relationships and prescribes dharma to truly bind a family together.

And dharma is all about giving, not taking. It is about duty to the world, not individual or family rights. It is about love for all, not power for a few. It is about affection, not domination. The epic indicates that the pressure of love and loyalty cannot bind family businesses and organizations. True unity can happen only when one abandons the power hierarchy, when one neither dominates nor gets dominated.

27

This was Ravana too

Ravana abducted Rama's wife, a crime for which he was killed by Rama himself. So says the Ramayana. The epic makes Ravana the archetypical villain. And since Rama is God for most Hindus, Ravana's actions make him the Devil incarnate. This justifies the annual burning of his effigy on the Gangetic plains during the festival of Dassera.

But on the hills of Rishikesh or in the temple of Rameswaram, one hears the tale of how Rama atoned for the sin of killing Ravana. Why should God atone for killing a villain? One realizes that like most things Hindu, the Ramayana is not as simplistic and pedestrian an epic as some are eager to believe.

Ravana was a Brahmin, the son of Rishi Vaishrava, grandson of Pulatsya. Rama, though God incarnate, was born in a family of Kshatriyas. In the caste hierarchy, Rama was of lower rank. As a Brahmin, Ravana was custodian of Brahma-gyan (the knowledge of God). Killing him meant Brahma-hatya-paap, the sin of Brahminicide, that Rama had to wash away through penance and prayer. Another reason why this atonement was important was because Ravana was Rama's guru.

The story goes that after firing the fatal arrow on the battlefield of Lanka, Rama told his brother, Lakshmana, 'Go to Ravana quickly before he dies and request him to share whatever knowledge he can. A brute he may be, but he is also a great scholar.' The obedient Lakshmana rushed across the battlefield to Ravana's side and whispered in his ear, 'Demon-king, do not let your knowledge die with you. Share it with us and wash away your sins.' Ravana responded by simply turning away. An angry Lakshmana went back to Rama. 'He is as arrogant as he always was, too proud to share anything.' Rama comforted his brother and asked him softly, 'Where did you stand while asking Ravana for knowledge?' 'Next to his head so that I hear what he had to say clearly.' Rama smiled, placed his bow on the ground and walked to where Ravana lay. Lakshmana watched in astonishment as his divine brother knelt at Ravana's feet. With palms joined, with extreme humility, Rama said, 'Lord of Lanka, you abducted my wife, a terrible crime for which I have been forced to punish you. Now you are no more my enemy. I bow to you and request you to share your wisdom with me. Please do that, for if you die without doing so, all your wisdom will be lost forever to the world.' To Lakshmana's surprise, Ravana opened his eyes and raised his arms to salute Rama. 'If only I had more time as your teacher than as your enemy. Standing at my feet as a student should, unlike your rude younger brother, you are a worthy recipient of my knowledge. I have very little time, so I cannot share much; but let me tell you one important lesson I have learnt in my life. Things that are bad for you seduce you easily; you run towards them impatiently. But things that are actually good for you fail to attract you; you shun them creatively, finding powerful excuses to justify your procrastination. That is why I was impatient to abduct Sita, but avoided meeting you. This is the wisdom of my life, Rama. My last words. I give it to you.' With these words, Ravana died.

With ten heads, twenty arms, a flying chariot and a city of gold, the mighty Ravana is without doubt a flamboyant villain. His sexual prowess was legendary. When Hanuman entered Lanka in search of Sita, he found the demon lord lying in bed surrounded by a bevy of beauties, women who had willingly abandoned their husbands. Rama, by comparison, seems boring—an upholder of rules who never does anything spontaneous or dramatic. He is the obedient son, always doing the right thing, never displaying a roving eye or a winsome smile. It is not difficult therefore to be a fan of Ravana, to be seduced by his power, to be enchanted by his glamour and to find arguments that justify his actions.

One can't help but wonder: Why does the poet Valmiki go out of his way to make his villain so admirable, so seductive, so enchanting?

Valmiki describes Ravana as the greatest devotee of Shiva. In many folk versions of the epic, such as Rama-kathas and Rama-kritis, we are informed that Ravana composed the Rudra Stotra in praise of Shiva, the ascetic god. He designed the lute known as Rudra-Veena using one of his ten heads as the lute's gourd, one of his arms as the beam and his nerves as the strings. The image of Ravana carrying Mount Kailas, with Shiva's family on top, is an integral part of Shiva temple art.

Perhaps, say some scholars, this expresses the legendary battle between Shiva worshippers and Vishnu worshippers. Rama, who is Vishnu on earth, kills Ravana, who is Shiva's devotee. But this argument falls flat when one is also told that Rama's trusted ally, Hanuman, is a form of Shiva himself. Valmiki is clearly conveying a more profound idea by calling Ravana a devotee of Shiva. And to understand the thought we have to dig a bit deeper.

Shiva is God embodying the principle of vairagya, absolute detachment. He demonstrates his disdain for all things material by smearing his body with ash and living in crematoriums. The material world does not matter to him. Ravana may be his great devotee, he may sing Shiva's praise and worship Shiva every day, but he does not follow the path of Shiva.

In reality, Ravana stands for everything that Shiva rejects. Ravana is fully attached to worldly things. He always wants what others have. He never built the city of gold—he drove out his brother, Kubera, and took over the kingdom of Lanka.

Why did he abduct Sita? Avenging his sister's mutilation was but an excuse; it was the desire to conquer the heart of a faithful wife. And during the war, he let his sons die and his brothers die before entering the battlefield himself.

Ravana has ten pairs of eyes, which means he can see more. Ravana has ten sets of arms, which means he can do more. Ravana has ten heads, which means he can think more. And yet, this man with a superior body and superior mind submits to the basest of passions. Despite knowing the Vedas and worshipping Shiva, he remains a slave of his senses and a victim of his own ego. He arrogantly shows off his knowledge of detachment but is not wise enough to practise detachment. Deluded, he gives only lip service to Shiva. This pretender is therefore killed by Rama who, like Shiva, is another form of God.

28

Becoming a leader

When commenting on the great Indian epic, the Mahabharata, people often point to the question raised by Draupadi: 'Does a man who has gambled himself have the right to gamble his wife?' But very few have asked the question: Does a king have the right to gamble his kingdom? What gives the Pandavas, in general, and Yudhishthira, in particular, the right to gamble his kingdom? A king is not the owner of the kingdom; he is its custodian.

If the kingdom is a cow that gives milk, the king is the cowherd. That is the traditional model of a leader in Hindu mythology. The king takes care of the kingdom and the kingdom nourishes him. He defends the kingdom and the kingdom empowers him. A cowherd cannot exist without a cow and a cow isn't safe without a cowherd. It's a symbiotic relationship. This is the essence of a king's role: to protect the cow, help it produce more calves, enable her to multiply and thrive and in the process create more cowherds. This is growth—growth for the cow and growth for the cowherd.

In the Mahabharata, there is a great debate on who should be king. Should kingship be determined by bloodline or meritocracy? After much debate and discussion and violence, which even involves an assassination attempt against the Pandavas, it is decided to divide the lands. The Pandavas get the underdeveloped half called Khandavaprastha, while their cousins, the Kauravas, get the prosperous city of Hastinapur. With the help of Krishna, the Pandavas transform Khandavaprastha into a great city called Indraprastha, which becomes the envy of the world. With the help of Krishna, the Pandavas even become kings. But then Krishna leaves, and in his absence, they gamble the kingdom away. It is almost as if, while they have the capacity to be kings, they lack the attitude of kingship.

And so, Krishna offers them no reprieve when they have to suffer twelve years of exile in the forest, living in abject poverty, followed by a year of humiliation when the former kings live in hiding as servants in another king's palace. In this time there are tales of how each brother gets a lesson in humility and patience. In one episode, the brothers reach a lake where a heron warns them against drinking the water until they answer its question; the impatient Pandavas drink nevertheless and die, all except Yudhishthira. Yudhishthira pauses, answers the questions and is then allowed to drink. This displays a shift in character. The man who, without thinking, gambled away his kingdom, is now ready to pause and think, question his actions and listen to good counsel before taking an action. He is suddenly more patient and prudent.

The heron then tells Yudhishthira that only one of his brothers will be brought back from the dead. He is asked to choose. 'Save Nakula,' he says. 'Why a weak stepbrother,' asks the heron, 'when you might as well save a strong brother like Bhima or a skilled one like Arjuna?' To this Yudhishthira says, 'My father had two wives. I, the son of his first wife Kunti, am alive. Let one son of the second wife Madri live too.' Here again we see a transformation. Nakula was the first of the five brothers to be gambled away in the game of dice. Thus, the unwanted stepbrother, who mattered least in the gambling hall, matters most in the forest. Yudhishthira has learnt the lessons of Raj-dharma, that it is not due to his greatness and grandeur that the crown is placed on his head. He exists for others; he exists for the weakest in his kingdom; he exists to help the helpless. Otherwise his kingdom is no different from the jungle where might is right. Otherwise he is no different from an alpha male.

Krishna, the supreme divine cowherd, thus acts as a coach in the Mahabharata. He is not king as in his previous life of Rama (whose story is told in the Ramayana). Here he plays lowly roles as cowherd and charioteer, but acts as a kingmaker. He knows that it is not just about skill alone (turning the wilderness into a rich kingdom). It is about attitude. And to shift attitude, sometimes, one has to be dragged through misery—thirteen years of forest exile.

Lessons from the ghost

A sorcerer once requested the legendary King Vikramaditya of Ujjain to fetch him a Vetal or ghost that hung upside down, like a bat, from the branches of a tree that stood in the middle of a crematorium. Not wanting to disappoint anyone who approached him, Vikramaditya immediately set out for the crematorium, determined to fetch the Vetal. 'Make sure you do not talk to him. If you speak, he will slip away from your grasp,' warned the sorcerer.

Vikramaditya entered the crematorium, found the tree and the Vetal hanging upside down from its branches. He caught the ghost, pulled it down and made his way back to the city when the ghost started chatting with him, telling him all kinds of things, annoying him, yelling into his ears, cursing him, praising him, anything to make him talk, but Vikramaditya refused to succumb to these tricks.

Finally, the Vetal told Vikramaditya a story, a case study, one might say, and at the end of it asked the king a question: 'If you are indeed the wise Vikramaditya, as you claim to be, you should know the answer to the riddle. But how will I know if you are truly he, unless you speak? And if you choose to stay silent, I am free to assume I have been caught by a commoner, a pretender, a mimic!' Too arrogant to be called a commoner, the king gave the answer. And it was a brilliant answer, one that made the Vetal gasp in admiration. And then he slipped away and went back to hang upside down from the branches of the tree in the middle of the crematorium.

So Vikramaditya had to walk back to the tree once again and pull the Vetal down once again. Once again the Vetal told him a story with a question at the end. Once again the Vetal told the king, 'If you are indeed the wise Vikramaditya, as you claim to be, you should know the answer to the riddle. But how will I know if you are truly he, unless you speak? And if you choose to stay silent, I am free to assume I have been caught by a commoner, a pretender, a mimic!' Once again the arrogant king gave the answer. Once again the Vetal gasped in admiration. And once again he slipped away.

This happened twenty-four times. The twenty-fifth time, a tired and exasperated Vikramaditya sighed in relief. He had succeeded. 'Have you really?' asked the Vetal. 'How do you know the answers you gave the previous times were right? Each decision was subjective, not objective. You thought you were right, and so you spoke. Now you are not sure of the answer, and so remain silent. This silence will cost you dear.

You will succeed in taking me to the sorcerer who will use his magic to make me his genie and do his bidding. His first order for me will be to kill you. So you see, Vikramaditya, as long as you kept answering my questions, rightly or wrongly, you were doing yourself a favour. You had to keep chasing me, but you stayed king. Now that you doubt yourself and stay silent, you are sure to end up dead.'

At the moment of decision-making, decisions are not right or wrong. They are right or wrong only in hindsight. He who takes decisions proactively, he who is not afraid to let the Vetal slip away, he who knows that life is about solving one problem after another, is Vikramaditya.

To improve decision making, Vikramaditya has to visit the crematorium, where the past hangs upside down like ghosts, and confront the Vetal. This is where learning takes place. This is where he hones his skills. The Vetal is the mentor, the trainer, the coach, the teacher, the guru, who presents the past as case studies and asks questions in the form of riddles and puzzles. Does the Vetal know the answer?

Maybe yes, maybe no. It does not matter. What matters is that Vikramaditya answers the questions and solves the problems. Every answer, every solution is subjective; only time will reveal if it is right and wrong. If Vikramaditya refuses to answer, he will end up destroying himself and his kingdom. A leader matters only as long as he seeks to solve problems.

Vikramaditya must always go to Vetal; the Vetal must never go to Vikramaditya. Vetal is Saraswati. Unlike Lakshmi and

Durga which can be given, Saraswati cannot be given. She has to be taken.

The crematorium is not a place where business happens, but it is here that the mind is expanded and beliefs are clarified. It is a place of new ideas, new thoughts, new frameworks that facilitate decision making. The more Vikramaditya visits the crematorium, the more he expands his mind, the more he gains Saraswati and the more attractive he becomes to power and prosperity, Durga and Lakshmi.

The process of gaining Saraswati is twofold. There is the outer voice called smriti and the inner voice called shruti. Smriti means that which can be remembered, hence transmitted. Shruti means that which can only be heard but cannot be transmitted.

What a teacher teaches a student, what is passed on through texts and puzzles and riddles and questions and case studies is just smriti. These can be parroted and passed on. These can be mouthed to impress people.

But real learning happens when the aspirant listens to his own voice, the inner voice of his mind. This is the only voice we hear. This is shruti. Only when smriti provokes shruti do we internalize wisdom. It becomes part of us. When this happens, we do not have to provide references for our knowledge ('This idea comes from that teacher'). We become the source of the knowledge ('This is my idea').

Books and lectures are smriti; they can be remembered and passed on. The reader or listener can allow it to provoke shruti. Only when they listen to their inner voice and truly 'get it' will this knowledge of the past transform into timeless wisdom. The way to this is to introspect on it personalize it, rather than intellectualize it. Frameworks appear when we see the mirror and are comfortable with the reflection.

As long as frameworks are meant to change the world, not ourselves, Saraswati will remain Vidya-Lakshmi, skill that grants prosperity but not peace. We will stay trapped in Swarga, like Indra, eternally on a shaky throne. We will never find Vaikuntha, where Lakshmi sits at our feet, and we always enjoy the rhythmic swing of the waves.

Every king whose rule extends up to the horizon, the Chakravarti, is no different from the Kupmanduka, the frog in the well. The walls of his kingdom define his well. However great the size may be, it is but a drop in the canvas of infinity. There is always scope to grow, outgrow the animal within, stop chasing Durga and Lakshmi and make them chase him instead. For this he has to cut his head.

Vetal cuts the head. Shruti cuts the head. Cutting of the head is a metaphor for intellectual as well as emotional growth. Intellectual growth may make us more skilled and less insecure, but it does not enable us to empathize. The point is not to be knowledgeable; the point is to be wise. And in India, wisdom happens when knowledge combines with empathy, gyan with karuna.

30

Last hymn of the Rig Veda

The Rig Veda has over a thousand hymns (sukta) that are arranged in ten chapters (mandala). The first and the tenth mandalas have precisely 191 hymns, indicating that the arrangement of hymns is not random, but deliberate. This organization of hymns is attributed to Vyasa.

Internal evidence in the Rig Veda suggests that originally there were many tribes and clans in the region now known as Punjab. But 3,000 years ago, one tribe dominated: the Kurus, also known as the Bharatas, under the leadership of one Sudas, who was supported by a sage called Vashishtha. He defeated the ten kings who were supported by Vishwamitra. Vashishtha and Vishwamitra were bitter rivals, an idea that germinates into a long narrative thread in the Puranas, composed much later. The 'battle of ten kings' perhaps inspired the later-day epic, the Mahabharata.

Perhaps the war was inconclusive, or so terrible for either side that it was necessary for the victor to bring together the brutalized sides to agree on a common way forward. This led to the composition and/or selection of the final hymn that unites the divided. The victory also perhaps marked the migration from the rivers in the Punjab region to the Gangetic plains.

Of course this is all speculation, as Vedic hymns are tough to translate. One is never sure what to take literally, what to take metaphorically, or symbolically. But what is interesting is the value placed on being united for the common good.

The hymn of eight lines states, and I paraphrase:

- Over and over, fire god, you gather what is precious for your friend
- You who stand in the path of libation, bring goods to us
- Assemble, speak together, let our thoughts agree
- As gods once came together to receive their portion
- Common in utterance, common in assembly, common in thought and feeling
- I hereby utter a common purpose and make a common oblation on your behalf
- Common is your resolve, your heart joined in one accord
- United in thoughts, so that it will go well for you together

The hymn reminds us of the fragmentation of every society, every family even. People have different ideas and drift away. Rather than collaborate, we combat. And we see this all around us as the European Union crumbles, as the

American president becomes belligerent, as states in India challenge the centre, as opposition refuses to work with the government, as the prime minister prefers to talk at the Parliament rather than to it. As people drift away or break asunder, it is time to sing hymns that motivate them to come closer together, like this, the final hymn of the Rig Veda.

The very first hymn of the Rig Veda is also an invocation to the fire god, Agni, who is seen as the mouth of the gods, through whom our offerings and petitions reach Indra and the other celestial devas, such as Varuna and Mitra and Soma. But while the first hymn is clearly a private individual exercise, the last seems to be one inviting others to join in. Could this be the first Vedic anthem, a call to unite? We can only speculate.

31

Science and the rishi

A minister recently allegedly told scientists in the defence industry to be like rishis. He was referring to the story of Sage Dadhichi who gave up his body so that his bones could be used to make the vajra weapon for Indra, king of the gods. But who were the rishis? Were they scientists or sorcerers or seers? Television would like us to believe that the rishis had a dress code: white or orange robes, beards and a Gandalf-like staff. Our knowledge of the rishis comes from the Vedas, composed 4,000 years ago, and the Puranas, which were composed over 1,000 years ago.

Science as a discourse is only 500 years old and we often confuse science with religion. This is why many people who 'believe' in science insist on being 'atheists', while there are many scientists who have no problem with keeping an image of Ganesha in their laboratories. Science is about facts.

Religion is about truth. The two are not the same. Science is based on measurement. Religion is based on experiences that are, by definition, not measurable. They are two ways of approaching reality, neither is superior nor inferior. When somebody asks whether yoga is scientific, it must be clarified that yoga is popular for the sublime 'experience' it offers, not because it is based on 'measurable provable facts'. The experience does not care for the measurements and measurement does not indicate experiences.

The word 'rishi' is rather mysterious. But some etymologists have traced it to the word 'drishti' or seeing. The rishis were thus seers: those who saw more than others. In the Vedas, they are often called 'kavi' or poets, those who questioned and wondered. The sound 'ka' refers to interrogation, and so interrogative pronouns such as 'what' and 'why' are derived from this sound. Ka is also the name by which the divine is addressed in the Vedas. They were interested in inquiry (mimansa), who 'heard' the chants that we now know as Vedic mantras. Is that a metaphor for inspiration? Or is it the humility of scholars who never attributed any discovery to themselves? Or is it indicative of a mystical experience, or maybe an extraterrestrial one, as some would like to believe?

Did rishis include women? When was the last time you saw a visualization of the Sapta Rishis, the seven sages of lore, including a single woman? Photographs of Indian scientists, like the ones involved in the Mars mission, included quite a few women dressed in sarees and with flowers in their hair. They were comfortable in their femininity, unlike many women in the corporate world—especially those at the junior level—who feel that the only way to show they are serious about their jobs is by downplaying their femininity. We can point to women who composed Vedic hymns, such as Lopamudra, and call them rishis, but that's more like a face-saving argument, rather than indicative of a trend.

In the Puranas, rishis are important narrative devices, as their curses and boons give rise to twists in the plot. Durvasa curses Indra to lose his wealth and splendour while he gives Kunti the boon to call any deva at will and have a child by him. Many of them are married: Gautama is with Ahalya, Vashishtha is with Arundhati, Atri with Anasuya and Agastya with Lopamudra. In fact, when they try to be celibate, Indra sends apsaras to seduce them. Holding of semen gave men supernatural powers known as 'siddhi', a popular theme in stories of the medieval Nath-jogis, which is why celibacy is valorized by our scientific gurus today.

32

The other wives

veryone knows that the five Pandava brothers in the epic Mahabharata shared a wife called Draupadi. What most people do not know is that each of the brothers had other wives too.

In fact, the first brother to get married was not Arjuna or the eldest, Yudhishthira, but the mighty Bhima. After the Kauravas attempted to kill the Pandavas by setting their palace (made of lac) on fire, the Pandavas hid in the forest, disguised as the sons of a Brahmin widow. During this time, Bhima killed many rakshasas, such as Baka and Hidimba. Hidimba's sister, impressed by his strength, chose him as husband and they had a son called Ghatotkacha.

Even before this, according to folk tales in Rajasthan and Odisha, Bhima had married a Naga woman. When the Kauravas tried to poison him and drown him in a river, he was saved by Ahuka, a Naga, and taken to the realm of the serpents, where he was given a wife. From that union was born a child called Bilalsena, who played a role in the war later on. In variants of this legend Bilalsena, also known as Barbareeka, was the son of Ghatotkacha, and hence was the grandson of Bhima, not son.

The brothers agreed that Draupadi would stay with one brother for a year before moving to the next one, a shrewd move to prevent jealousy and to identify the paternity of Draupadi's children. In the four years in between, each brother spent time with another wife.

Yudhishthira married Devika, the daughter of Govasana of the Saivya tribe, and begat upon her a son called Yaudheya. Bhima married Valandhara, the daughter of the king of Kashi, and begat upon her a son named Sarvaga. Nakula married Karenumati, the princess of Chedi, and begat upon her a son named Niramitra. Sahadeva obtained Vijaya, the daughter of Dyutimat, the king of Madra, and begat upon her a son named Suhotra. All these wives lived with their sons in the house of their fathers.

When Draupadi agreed to be the common wife, her condition was that she would share her household with no other woman. In other words, disregarding popular practice of the times, the Pandavas could not bring their other wives to Indraprastha. Arjuna, however, succeeded in bringing one wife in. She was Krishna's sister, Subhadra. And with a little advice from Krishna, she was able to trick her way into the household.

Though Draupadi's favourite, Arjuna had the most

number of wives amongst all the brothers. The story goes that Arjuna once entered Draupadi's chamber while she was with Yudhishthira. To atone for this trespassing, he went on a 'pilgrimage'. During this time he married many women.

In the classical Sanskrit retelling, Arjuna married the Naga Ulupi, Princess Chitrangada of Manipur and finally Krishna's sister Subhadra during this pilgrimage. But in Tamil retellings of the Mahabharata, he married seven women in total. One of them was a warrior woman called Ali who refused to marry him but Arjuna was so besotted that he sought Krishna's help. Krishna turned him into a snake and he slipped into Ali's bed at night and frightened her into becoming his wife. Some say he forced her to be his wife, as he managed to spend the night in bed with her in the form of a snake. This clandestinely erotic folk tale alludes to Pisacha-vivaha, or the marriage by way of ghosts, that is condemned in the Puranas.

Thus, the world of the Mahabharata very comfortably refers to polyandry (many husbands for one woman) as well as polygyny (many wives for one man). What is interesting to note is that most storytellers are embarrassed only by the former than the latter; hence there are tales to 'explain' Draupadi's many husbands, but none to explain each Pandava's other wives.

33

The strange tale of Oghavati

Oghavati was the wife of one Sudarshan and Bhishma tells her story to the Pandavas in the Anushasan Parva while explaining ethics and morality. While stepping out of the house, her husband told her, 'Should a guest arrive in my absence, take care of all his needs.' While he was away a guest did arrive, but his needs were a bit excessive. He wanted to have sex with her. Oghavati agreed. And while the two were thus engaged, Sudarshan returned home. 'Wife, where are you?' he asked. Oghavati was too shy to reply. So the guest shouted from inside, 'She is busy with me on your bed, attending to my desires.' Sudarshan replied, 'Oh, okay. I will wait outside until you are done.' Eventually Oghavati and the guest came out and the guest blessed the couple for their generous hospitality. The guest, Bhishma reveals, was none other than Dharma, god of righteous conduct.

This story can be rather discomforting. The story challenges most modern notions of ethics and morality. It challenges the notions of marital fidelity and appropriate social conduct. It seems like a tale of a primitive society where sex hospitality was a norm. A feminist may argue that it shows either freedom of women or subjugation of women as per the whims of the husband. A moralist may argue that this is a tale of the Kali Yuga, when morals collapse. But according to the Mahabharata, which describes a war on the eve of Kali Yuga, this story belongs to an earlier, more proper age.

There is much confusion between the words ethics and morality. Ethics comes from the Greek word 'ethos', which is more social in nature, and refers to behaviours that establish a noble society. Morality comes from the Latin word 'moralitas', which is more personal in nature, and refers to behaviours that establish good character. In the original sense of the term, ethics referred greatly to the notion of hospitality: the way a human being treated strangers enabled one to judge how noble a society was. The idea that 'guest is God' is a key thought that resonates across the Ramayana and the Mahabharata. In the Bible, Abraham, father of the Jewish, Christian and Islamic faiths, was renowned for his hospitality. So the hospitality of Sudarshan and Oghavati is indeed commendable and ethical. But is it moral?

And it is here that things get a bit tough philosophically. Indian philosophy has always celebrated detachment over attachment. To equate the notion of 'yours' with 'you' is frowned upon. Your property or your spouse, or even your body (different types of 'yours') is not an extension of 'you'. In fact, any proprietorship is seen as maya – the great delusion.

So the question is: As wife, is Oghavati the property of Sudarshan? Can Sudarshan say 'Oghavati is "mine"' and claim rights over her? If yes, he becomes a patriarch and then he can order her around. If no, she is free to do as she pleases. So is Oghavati doing her wifely duty, obeying her husband, surrendering all free will, or is she freely, without compulsion, being hospitable without feeling exploited? Where does one draw the line?

These are the ideas that the Mahabharata presents to us. No clear answer is given. They are not prescriptions of behaviour. They are supposed to be reflections on beliefs.

34

If you love me…

Emotional blackmail perhaps began with Kaikeyi, who used it to get her way with Dasharatha in the Ramayana. Or maybe Duryodhana, who used emotional blackmail to manipulate Karna in the Mahabharata. Even perhaps Krishna when he told Arjuna, 'If you love me, pick up your bow and fight your enemy.'

Naturally, it has made its way to Indian families. The mother says, 'If you love me, you will finish all the food on the plate.' Then the father says, 'If you love me, you will study hard.' Then the aunt says, 'If you love me, you will not marry that girl you chose.' Then the uncle says, 'If you love me, you will marry this girl we chose.' Lovers often say to each other, 'If you love me, you will give up your job/religion/family/life.'

Religions have long used this strategy. Evangelists go around saying, 'If you love the Lord, you will hate homosexuals and those who support abortions.' Religious sects say, 'If you love the guru, you will make that donation regularly.' Political parties tell voters, 'If you care for the minorities/Hindus/Dalits/social justice, you will vote for us.'

So it had to happen. 'If you care for your country, you have to watch a television show.' The ultimate measure of patriotism driven by consumption economics!

Animals do not emotionally blackmail, though some dog lovers reluctantly admit being controlled by the weepy whines of their pets. Humans set themselves up for emotional blackmail. It is rooted in the human desire to be validated by those around us. We may be rich/honest/brave/patriotic, but we need someone else to validate it. And people take advantage of this yearning for validation. They turn into judges and define evaluation measures that usually benefit them. As long as we grant such people the power to judge us, we remain at the receiving end.

But then one day the child grows up. Refuses to eat that food the mother forces him to eat, or marry the girl the family chooses for him, or take up a career that meets with family approval. Rather than submit to family pressures, he follows his own heart. He is accused of being the unfaithful son, the home wrecker, even the evil one. But he does not succumb. He does not need their judgement to validate himself. He makes his own path, knowing fully well that he loves his parents, even if they are manipulative control freaks, even if they are unable to love him for not being their perfect obedient child.

Emotional blackmailers, despite their avowed declaration of noble intentions ('I am doing it for your own good'), are usually self-absorbed. They fail to understand the other. They never ask, 'Why is he not doing what I feel is good for him?' If they did, they would understand something more about the human condition and about themselves. There would be a bit more affection and empathy for the failings of humankind, and less smug sanctimony.

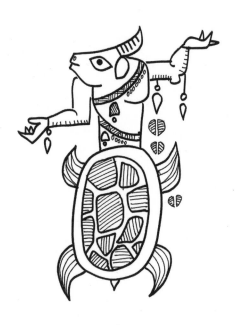

35

How we read mythology

It all started with the Harry Potter series. Suddenly, magic became a cool world amongst children. And when Indian children started looking for magic in their own backyard they rediscovered mythology, a world of fantastic beings who do fantastic things. But what is interesting is how these mythological stories are being interpreted nowadays. It reveals the power of European and American thought processes in the Indian mind.

I remember meeting an earnest dancer who told me, rather confidently, how Rama was an Aryan invader who was there to destroy south Indian dark-skinned rakshasa tribes, just as before him devas lead by Indra destroyed the cities of north Indian—again dark-skinned—asuras. This dancer now wanted me to explain the Ramayana within the boundaries that he had drawn, boundaries that he was convinced were objective and true.

I did not have the heart to tell him that this reading of mythology along racial lines was made popular in the early part of the twentieth century by British Orientalists, who were struggling to understand India and Indians, who seemed relatively indifferent to their own history. They popularized this 'racial' and 'invasion' theory. It reaffirmed their faith in the superiority of white people. It also justified their rule of India, by declaring that the dominant communities of India, the Muslim rulers of various states, and their Brahmin ministers, were all descendants of earlier invaders. Was this a conscious strategy or a genuine theory, since then rejected? We will never know. Of course, we can argue over it relentlessly, over a cup of tea.

Then I received an email from an angry social activist who asked why Hindus worship a man who abandoned his pregnant wife in the forest. I realized, since judgement had been pronounced, I was suddenly being asked to 'defend' Rama, as I am a mythologist and a Hindu. The parameters of discussion had been defined by the email writer and thus he was unwilling to listen to anything that demanded the parameters be changed.

This reading of Indian epics like the Ramayana using the lens of 'fairness and justice' has been popularized by American scholars. America prides itself as the first nation on earth to challenge feudalism and monarchy and establish a new governance model based on democracy. And so American scholars, willy-nilly, see red whenever they see a 'model king'. Rama is thus fodder for the activist, easy to rip apart. So is Krishna, who bends and breaks rules to establish dharma, what Europeans deemed to mean 'righteousness', a mistranslation that continues to be upheld by Indian writers and even journalists. That this annoys the right-wing fanatics gives them further fuel. No sensible discussion is possible.

To appreciate Hindu mythology, we have to agree to Hindu assumptions. That is difficult, since the modern world is firmly based on Western assumptions. The Hindu assumption is one of rebirth. Thus, the Ramayana and the Mahabharata are being played out on a canvas where every event is a play of other events in past lives. So words like victims, villains, heroes cannot be applied easily. These words belong to finite linear world views, like in Greek mythology. Rama and Krishna are not heroes or superheroes; they are avatars, which has a very specific meaning that makes no sense in the Western world. Such paradigm-challenging conversations are rare because we have been conditioned to receive and digest only simple, or rather simplistic explanations that simply reaffirm our firmly held assumptions.

36

What's your sanskar?

Don't use the word culture. Use the word sanskar. And see how the organization responds. The two words, rather spontaneously, evoke very different reactions amongst Indians who straddle the modern and traditional worlds continuously.

When we use the word 'culture', we immediately have images of cultural programmes held in schools and at associations where children do folk dance and sing classical songs. It's all about performance of some traditional art form. But is that all culture is? A performance meant to entertain us during festivals? Something nostalgic and quaint, far removed from the daily grind of the workplace? It is at best an ornament, good to have, not essential.

When we use the word 'sanskar', the reaction is rather different. For sanskar refers to upbringing in India. It is the key performance indicator of parenting for most Indians. It is an indicator of family values. It shows how civilized and cultured we are.

The word sanskar is a wordplay typical of Sanskrit. It is a combination of three roots: First: 'saras', which means fluid. Second: 'sama', which means cyclical or closed loop. Third: 'ka', which means questioning, an indicator of humanity as well as divinity in the Vedas. Sanskara is then how the human mind makes sense of this cyclical world of birth and death, which we all inhabit. It is an indicator of the value placed on human existence by the family one belongs to. Every organization needs sanskar to show the world whether it is connected to society at large and to the environment as a whole.

In India, sanskar is created by simply following rites of passage, also called sanskar. In other words, both the means to create culture and culture itself mean the same thing. Typical sanskars are marriage, childbirth, piercing the child's ear, tonsure of the child's hair, the first eating of solid food, first day at school and finally, death. Sanskars are also linked to how festivals are celebrated; how food is served; how the house is kept; how daughters, sons, elders, guests, servants, strangers and enemies are treated. Most rituals, like all rituals, have symbolic meaning or have no meaning at all. The action needs to be performed, but what is key to the ritual performance is the underlying emotion of the action—the bhaav. Ritual with bhaav is advised. Ritual without bhaav is tolerated. Bhaav without ritual is unperceivable.

Modern management ignores bhaav, as that cannot be

measured. It focuses on rules (niti) and tradition (riti). In this approach, culture becomes not an expression of ideas but a rigid code of conduct that the modern man has to revolt against in order to be free. At best, it becomes something to turn to nostalgically. And it is this approach to culture that is increasingly becoming popular.

In the Puranas, Shiva is unable to appreciate the sanskar of his father-in-law Daksha, for Shiva values emotions more than rituals while Daksha values rituals over emotion. The confrontation is violent.

Culture is an outcome of any human interaction. There cannot be an organization without culture. There are levels of human culture, of course, in the Puranas:

- The default culture (Level 0) is the animal culture where natural instincts (prakriti) are indulged, where might is right, where domination and conflict thrive and it is all about packs and herds and grabbing nourishment and security. This is seen in organizations where there is breakdown of leadership.

- The next type of culture (Level 1) is one where the human-animal is domesticated using rules and rewards and recognition. This is seen in highly controlled workspaces.

- Another type of culture is one where one abandons all things material and gives up all relationship—the monastic culture (Level 2).

- Then comes the ecosystem (Level 3) where people are continuously encouraged, not compelled, to be sensitive to others voluntarily for their own emotional and intellectual well-being. This is sanskriti, where everyone knows how to behave with men, women, those older and younger, those related and unrelated, strangers and colleagues. This is aspirational.

The questions to ponder over are: Is culture critical? Do modern institutions think of culture only when the going is good? Do they see culture as a lever that enables success? More importantly, if the going is bad, does culture matter? Will culture help tide over a crisis, or will it be the cause of crisis?

In stories, sanskar is not always profitable. In the Ramayana, Surpanakha's sanskar allows her to approach a married man for pleasure; Sita's sanskar compels her to risk personal security and feed a hungry sage who turns out to be a demon; Rama's sanskar forces him to abandon his beloved innocent wife as she is deemed a queen of stained reputation. In the Mahabharata, Draupadi abandons all sanskar and becomes violent and bloodthirsty when she is publicly abused, and all family decorum is abandoned by her vile brothers-in-law, the Kauravas. Yet, this very same Draupadi recalls sanskar when she forgives her sister-in-law Duhshala's lecherous husband, Jayadratha, even though he tries to abduct her.

As long as culture is treated synthetically as an ornament

of the good times, it can never ever add real value. Only when we recognize culture as sanskar, an indicator of our humanity, does it become critical to organizational survival.

37

Search for Rama's ring

One day, Rama was informed that it was time for him to die. He had no problem with that. He understood that creatures who take birth have to experience death. 'Let Yama come to me. It is time for me to return to my heavenly abode, Vaikuntha,' he said. But Yama dared not enter Ayodhya. Yama, the god of death, was afraid of Hanuman who guarded the gates of Rama's palace and was clear that no one would take Rama away from him.

To allow Yama's entry, it was necessary to distract Hanuman. So Rama dropped his ring into a crack in the palace floor and requested Hanuman to fetch it. Hanuman reduced himself to the size of a beetle and entered the crack, only to discover that it was no crack but the entrance to a tunnel that led to Nag-lok, the land of serpents. Hanuman met Vasuki, king of serpents, there and informed him of his mission.

Vasuki took Hanuman to the centre of Nag-lok where stood a mountain of rings! 'There you will surely find Rama's ring,' said Vasuki. Hanuman wondered how he would do that. It was like finding a needle in a haystack. But to his delight, the first ring he picked up was Rama's ring. To his astonishment, even the second ring he picked up was Rama's ring. In fact, all the rings that made up the mountain of rings were Rama's ring. 'What is the meaning of this?' he wondered.

Vasuki smiled and said, 'This world we live in goes through cycles of life and death. Each life cycle of the world is called a kalpa. Each kalpa is composed of four yugas or quarters. In the second quarter or Tret Yuga, Rama takes birth in Ayodhya. Then one day his ring falls from earth into the subterranean realm of serpents through a tunnel. A monkey follows it, and Rama dies up there. So it has been for hundreds of thousands of kalpas. All these rings testify to that fact. The mountain keeps growing as more rings fall. There is enough space for the rings of the future Rama.'

Hanuman realized that his entry into Nag-lok and his encounter with this mountain of rings was no accident. It was Rama's way of telling him that he could not stop death from coming. Rama would die. The world would die. But like all things, Rama would be reborn each time the world is reborn. So it would be forever.

This cyclical view of life is the essence of Indian thought. This was destroyed by the British and their linear view of life was adopted by everyone, including India's political parties.

That is why everyone wants to locate Rama in history and geography, and fights over dates and addresses.

For the Hindu mind, Rama is timeless and universal and so cannot be fettered to period or place. That is why the day of his birth is celebrated every year as spring gives way to summer. Every year he comes, every year he goes. But everyone has faith that he will keep coming back.

38

In justice we trust

In most courtrooms built in the colonial period, we see the image of a woman with a blindfold balancing scales in her arms. This is Lady Justice, based on a Greek goddess described in Hesiod's Theogony called Dike, daughter of Zeus, who is associated with human justice while her mother Themis is associated with divine justice. In art, she was shown bearing scales. Her Roman form, Justitia, was blindfolded. She was imagined as innocent-looking, throttling the ugly Adikia (injustice) and beating her with a stick, or killing her with a sword. The story goes that she lived with humans in the Golden and Silver Ages, when there were no wars. But then humans grew greedy and justice was forgotten and Dike ran away to be with her father, high on Mount Olympus, away from human corruption.

The idea of associating justice with scales is much older

though and can be traced to the Egyptian goddess of justice, Maat, and later Isis. The feather of Maat was used to weigh the heart of the dead, to see if they were worthy of entering the land of Osiris, or if a monster should simply eat them, depriving them of the afterlife. The idea spread from Egyptian mythology through Greek mythology to Christian mythology, with the archangel Michael often shown holding scales. Sin makes the heart heavy and causes the sinner to be cast in hell. The virtuous go to heaven.

Of course, in India, we are slowly resigning ourselves to the idea that the rich, the powerful, the famous are usually seen as innocent, and go to heaven. Allegedly, the judges of our courts seem eager to forgive, going through heaps and heaps of evidence to find a flaw either in data or process, a benefit of doubt denied to those without lawyers, without connections, without wealth. Perhaps that is why the blindfold. It must be frustrating for judges of lower courts to find their judgments being suspended and overturned by the judges of the 'higher' courts. A kind of judicial feudalism, if one thinks about it. But then criticizing courts is akin to blasphemy, for the courts and the judicial systems were designed based on assumptions of Abrahamic mythology, where fear of God's fire and brimstone is supposed to keep humanity from committing evil, and where God/Judge is never wrong.

The blindfold was meant to show equality before the law, as before the eyes of God, for did not Jehovah punish his prophet Moses and his king David for breaking just one law?

Humans hope for a world where the crime is seen without factoring in the estate or titles of the accused. But that remains more aspirational than real.

In many ancient societies, the stature of the man and woman is always considered while dispensing justice, looking at the larger narrative at stake. In many societies, if a rich man killed a poor man, the rich man was asked to pay the poor man a hefty fine, pragmatism thus overshadowing vengeance. In the Manu Smriti, caste determines the intensity of punishment. The scale of justice was, in many societies, meant to balance good deeds against the bad. If the good deeds were greater than the bad deeds, then there was a lesser punishment, as compared to when the bad deeds were greater than the good deeds. This accounting method of justice is found in many ancient societies, including India, where Chitragupta, the scribe of Yama, maintains an account of equity-generating actions (punya) and debt-generating actions (paap). This belief perhaps accounts for the temple-going and charitable deeds that the accused in India indulge in, rather publicly, before the Day of Judgement, when judges seem to be increasingly turned into loving saviours rather than upright angels, and the accuser, and the policemen, feel like idiots for trusting the system.

39

When a dog wept in Ayodhya

This story comes from the *Anand Ramayana*, attributed to Valmiki, and written in Sanskrit in the fifteenth century. Long after Rama became king and all was well with the world, a dog came crying before him. He has been struck by a priest because he had licked food from the priest's plate. Rama declared the priest guilty and asked the dog if he had any particular punishment for the priest. 'Make him the head of the temple.' Rama immediately agreed.

Everyone thought this was strange. The priest had wronged the dog and instead of being punished he had been promoted to the position of the head of a temple. What was the mystery?

So the dog explained, 'I too was once head of a temple. When you become the head of a temple, you become powerful, as everyone listens to you and your word is law. Then you become corrupt. And you do stupid things. And when you die, you are reborn as a dog. I want the priest who struck me to suffer the same fate as I did. I therefore want him to get a position of power and become corrupt.'

Whether we believe in rebirth or not, we all know power corrupts. But when we think of power, we think of politicians or policemen. But that is not the only seat of power. We can see that in cricket, both in the players and the mandarins of the game. Old, withered men clinging to power, transforming what is supposed to be fun and entertainment into a complex web of intrigue. And we see that in Bollywood, young starlets throwing tantrums once they become stars, actors who were humble before their break transforming into demanding monsters once they get their first hit. We see that in the corporate world, with CEOs behaving like maharajas, treating their organizations as private fiefdoms but spouting management mantras at all conferences.

Why do simple, decent human beings become corrupt? It's a question that begs to be asked. Is it genetic, considering that we do have concepts like sociopaths and psychopaths, popularized by television serials? Is it about upbringing: denial of love and attention to children? Is it about too much wealth or too little wealth? Is it just our inability to cope with success? Is it God-complex, suddenly believing that the world revolves around us? Is it Devil-complex, anger at the world that has treated us as nobodies for a very long time?

At the heart of corruption is deep loneliness, a sense of feeling exploited and unloved. And so we strike back with a vengeance, hurt the world before it hurts us, exploit the world before it exploits us. We want to feel safe. So we strike dogs, accusing them of licking utensils. We play politics and do everything in our power to become heads of temples. We are just not able to sit back, relax and enjoy the abundance that nature very spontaneously brings before us.

40

Time, timelessness and
the idea of charity

The Biblical or Abrahamic world view informs the Western view, just as the Hindu world view informs the Indian world view. The Bible speaks of a beginning and an end, Genesis and Apocalypse. Thus the Biblical world view is finite. The Vedas speak of a world that is anadi, without beginning, and without end, ananta. Thus the Hindu world view is infinite. What does this mean in the practical sense?

It means that the Biblical world view focuses on solving problems using material things that have a finite existence, while the Hindu world view focuses on solving problems using psychological ideas that challenge material finiteness. The Bible speaks of a Promised Land that will be granted to the chosen people. It also speaks of, 'Blessed are the poor for they shall inherit the earth'. The vocabulary is about having or not having. By contrast, the Ramayana and the Mahabharata end with Rama giving up his kingdom and walking into the River Sarayu and the Pandavas giving up their kingdom and walking up the Himalayas. It's all about letting go.

Western society focuses on the material more than the mental, because the material is empirical. Everything is viewed in terms of wealth, and holidays. He who has money to spend and time to enjoy is blessed indeed. Monastic orders in the West are therefore embracing poverty and serving the poor to uplift them from the status of 'have-nots' to 'haves'. Equality is about creating a world where there are no 'have-nots'.

In Indian thought, there is tension between 'bhoga' (satisfying hunger/desire) and 'yoga' (outgrowing hunger/desire). Those who chose the former path lived in human settlements and those who chose the latter path went into caves. Indian philosophy rejects the idea of equality, as it assumes that the world will always have 'haves' and 'have-nots' but as time passes, the 'haves' become 'have-nots' and the 'have-nots' become 'haves', and the wise discover that happiness follows when one outgrows the desire to have 'having' or the regret of 'not-having'.

This subtle difference is often overlooked by scholars who write about Indian or Western philosophy. The human mind refuses to accept rebirth, hence change. We think this moment is permanent. We use Western ideas as benchmarks and templates to explain Indian thought. This is evident in writings about Hindu philosophy in colonial times. There are strong attempts to explain Hindus to the West in Western terms: thus, there are concepts like the 'Gospel of the Gita' or the 'Hindu Church'.

Nowadays, there is great popularity amongst Hindu outfits to do 'seva' or serve people. The assumption is: If you want to be spiritual, you must serve people. Placed in a Biblical framework it makes sense, for it means you are aligning with God's commandments and following the path of love preached by Jesus. But in the Hindu framework, it becomes a bit problematic. For it is an act done to generate good karma: in other words, seva (service) for meva (fat). Thus, there is nothing unconditional or selfless about it.

In Sikhism, the gurus said that the person who gives service must thank the person who receives service. Why? Because the charity-giver gets credit while the charity-receiver gets bound in debt, or 'rin'. Debt fetters one to worldly life and becomes an obstacle to liberation, as one is obliged to repay debt in this or another lifetime.

In a global world order, we want to homogenize spirituality. And in the process of homogenizing spirituality, we try to standardize world views. More often than not, the world view adopted is the finite, time-bound Western one and not the infinite, timeless Indian one.

41

The good death

Euthanasia means a good death and is term used for an old or sick person voluntarily choosing death to relieve himself/herself of pain and suffering, either by refusing treatment or by asking the assistance of a doctor to facilitate his/her death, either actively (administering a poison, for example) or passively (not administering a treatment, for example). It's a highly controversial topic.

The roots of this controversy can be traced to nineteenth-century debates, which in turn can be traced to the Judeo-Christian-Islamic attitude towards suicide. In the Biblical world view suicide is self-murder, hence against the commandments of God, hence a sin. In Judaism, those who committed suicide were buried in a separate cemetery and denied proper burial rites. In Islam, Prophet Muhammad expressly forbade suicide and refused to bless the body of one who had done so. Since the British established the modern Indian legal system in India, their Christian belief manifested itself when those who attempted suicide were treated as criminals, rather than with compassion. It is this same root in Christian belief that made homosexuality illegal in our country.

Until the rise of Christianity, most cultures did not think nor harbour too much negative feeling about suicide or assisted suicide. For example, the Greeks were comfortable with the idea of consuming hemlock (a poison) to kill oneself. Socrates and Plato spoke of it matter-of-factly. The Romans were known to stab themselves rather than face dishonour. We hear of the famous suicides of Antony (by self-stabbing) and Cleopatra (who put her hand in a basket containing a poisonous snake). The Japanese turned the practice of suicide into an elaborate ritual called hara-kiri or seppuku, which was part of the bushido code of samurai warriors.

In Hinduism, there is no concept of commandments. And there is belief in rebirth. And so attitudes towards dying are very different. This is not the only life; this is but one of many lives. The human being is advised to divide his/her life into four parts: first as a student (brahmachari), then as a householder (grihasthi), then as a retired person (vanaprasthi) and finally as a hermit (sanyasi). In the first phase, he eats as much as he wants; in the second phase, he eats only as much as he needs, as he bears worldly responsibilities; in the third phase, he eats only half of what he ate as a householder and focuses on withdrawing form worldly responsibilities; and finally, he shuns food, focusing his mind on liberation from the cycle of birth and death. Thus, there is an implicit encouragement of voluntary death.

In the Mahabharata, the old parents of the Kauravas and the mother of the Pandavas go to the forest, where they are engulfed by a forest fire. The Pandavas themselves in their old age go to the Himalayas, where they fall to their death. Thus, they were exposing themselves to situations where the probability of death was high. They did not kill themselves but walked into situations were the probability of death was high, indicating their detachment from life.

In the Ramayana, after Sita enters the earth, Rama chooses to enter the River Sarayu and attains samadhi. Saints like Sant Dyaneshwara, who translated the Gita for the first time from Sanskrit to a regional language in the thirteenth century, also chose the path of samadhi. Rationalists view samadhi as a euphemism for voluntary suicide but devotees disagree, for suicide—because of the law—has a negative connotation to it, and suggests helplessness and weakness, when in fact those who practise samadhi are seen as wise and enlightened beings who use yogic practices to voluntarily leave their mortal bodies.

Voluntary suicide is explicitly embraced in Jainism where both the monk (shramana) and the commoner (shravaka) are encouraged to embrace death by gradual starvation, after fulfilling all worldly duties, and by cleansing the mind of all attachments. This practice is called santhara. Chandragupta

Maurya, grandfather of Ashoka the Great, embraced death in this way.

Buddhism does not encourage or discourage euthanasia, but seeks to appreciate the nature of suicide. If it is an outcome of ignorance, the future life is bound to be sorrowful. If it is an outcome of wisdom and detachment, as in case of the bhikkus Godhika and Vakkali, the future life may bring the promise of nirvana.

That being said, the concept of voluntary suicides can easily be misused, and India has seen this spectacularly in the practice of sati. What began allegedly as an attempt of women to protect themselves from abuse during wartime and for women to express their love for the husbands ended up as a tool to get rid of 'unwanted' widows. The only other option for them was exile to the widow houses of Mathura and Kashi. By glorifying sati, women were pressurized to kill themselves, enabling greedy relatives to lay claim to the properties left behind by their dead husbands. It is possible that those not wanting to care for old and sick people will misuse a law favouring euthanasia. But by disallowing euthanasia, the law can also end up amplifying the pain and suffering of many, in the name of imagined righteousness.

42

Violence and the Gita

Mahatma Gandhi found inspiration for his satyagraha or non-violent protest in the Gita. Bal Gangadhar Tilak, on the other hand, found in the Gita a justification of violence, if the intent and objective is righteous. So does the Gita preach violence or not?

I remember an essay on the Gita written by Wendy Doniger in which she spoke of how the Gita goes out of its way to justify violence. She also quoted Romila Thapar as to how the Buddha would have responded to Arjuna's crisis differently. You can imagine how this essay would upset many Hindus, especially those who keep telling their children how Hinduism preaches non-violence and hence, vegetarianism.

The contrast between Buddhism and Hinduism is stark. The founder of Buddhism walked away from his family and his kingdom to become a hermit who rejected desire, sex and violence. In contrast, Hinduism insisted that a man perform his duty based on caste rules. Whatever be his views on desire, sex and violence, he had to marry, produce children and take care of his family by pursuing the family profession. He who was born in a warrior family had to go to war and fight. He who was born in a butcher family had to slaughter animals for food. The Ramayana and the Mahabharata valorize not war so much as the pursuit of social obligation, even while engaging in long discussions on the morality of war.

At the heart of this controversy is the fundamental question: Is violence good or bad? To answer this question, we have to pay attention to the role of violence in nature and culture. In nature, animals survive by indulging in violence. Herbivores bite and tear plants. Carnivores hunt animals. Violence is used to establish the pecking order, mark territory and isolate mates. Culture is also established through violence. Forests are burned to create fields. Riverbanks are broken to create canals. Mountains are blasted to find minerals. Animals are castrated to serve as beasts of burden. Thus, violence is intrinsic to both nature and culture. Violence enables animals to find food. Humans use violence to generate wealth and lay claim to property.

Buddhism has a monastic tilt. A monk rejects wealth and property. So he rejects violence. But society is not made up of monks. How does one help people who have no choice but to participate in violence? How does one help a soldier who has to fight in a war or a policeman who has to catch a criminal? We may not use violence to offend, but we have to use violence to defend and survive. We do not like being at the receiving end of violence, but we do know that violence is sometimes necessary to create a civil society.

Today, Western media is horrified that its pacifist understanding of Buddhism, constructed by its dealings with the Dalai Lama, is being challenged by brutal violence perpetrated by Buddhist leaders in Myanmar and Sri Lanka. Here the question is not about outgrowing desire, it is about wealth and property, which are essential aspects of human existence. As long as we want wealth and property, there is no escaping violence. And violence thus perpetrated has consequences that we are obliged to suffer. The Gita recognizes this.

43

Forest and field in dharma discussion

 In the Sama Veda, the hymns of the Rig Veda are turned into melodies. These melodies are classified into two groups: aranya-gaye-gana or forest songs, and grama-gaye-gana or settlement songs. This divide plays a key role in the understanding of dharma.

Forest is the default state of nature. In the forest, there are no rules. The fit survive and the unfit die. The stronger, or the smarter, have access to food. The rest starve. There is no law, no authority, and no regulation. This is called 'matsya nyaya' or law of the fish, the Vedic equivalent of the law of the jungle. This is prakriti, visualized as Kali, the wild goddess who runs naked with unbound hair, of the Puranas.

Humans domesticate the forest to turn it into fields and villages for human settlement. Here, everything is tamed: plants, animals, even humans, bound by niti (rules), (riti) tradition, codes of conduct, duties and rights. Here, there is an attempt to take care of the weak and unfit. This is the hallmark of sanskriti or civilization, visualized as Gauri, the docile goddess who is draped in a green sari, and whose hair is tied with flowers, who takes care of the household.

The Ramayana tells the story of Rama who moves from Ayodhya, the settlement of humans, the realm of Gauri, into the forest, the realm of Kali. The Mahabharata tells the story of the Pandavas who are born in the forest, then come to Hastinapur, and then return to the forest as refugees, and then once again return to build Indraprastha, then yet again return to the forest as exiles, and finally, after the victory at war and a successful reign, they return to the forest following retirement.

As children, we are trained to live in society—that is brahmacharya. Then we contribute to society as householders—grihasthi. Later we are expected to leave for the forest—vanaprastha; and then comes the hermit life or sanyasa, when we seek the world beyond the forest.

According to the Buddhist Sarvastivadin commentary, Abhidharma-mahavibhasa-sastra, forest or vana, is one of the many etymologies of the word 'nirvana', the end of identity, prescribed by Buddhist scriptures, which is the goal of dhamma, the Buddhist way.

Rama lives in a city, and so does Ravana. But Rama follows rules. Ravana does not care for rules. In other words, Ravana follows matsya nyaya though he is a city dweller, a nagara-vasi. That is adharma. If Ravana uses force to get his way, Duryodhana uses his cunning, also focusing on the self rather than the other. That is adharma. Dharma is when we function for the benefit of others. It has nothing to do with rules. Which is why Krishna, the rule-breaker, is also upholding dharma, for he cares for the other.

In the forest, everyone is driven by self-preservation. Only humans have the wherewithal to enable and empower others to survive and thrive. To do so is dharma. It has nothing to do with rules or tradition. It is about being sensitive to, and caring for, the other. We can do this whether we are in the forest or in the city. And so it is in the vana or forest that Krishna dances with the gopikas, making them feel safe, even though they are out of their comfort zone.

Without appreciating the forest and the field, Kali and Gauri—the animal instinct and human capability—any discussion of dharma will be incomplete.

44

The complete man

There are two Krishnas. One lived in north India, in the Gangetic plains around Mathura, and later on the island of Dwaraka, off the Gujarat coast, in 3112 BCE. This was found on the basis of astronomical data found in the Mahabharata, undersea archaeological remains and the Indus seals that depict a man uprooting two trees, an event associated with Krishna lore. The other Krishna has lived in the heart and minds of devotees for the past 2,000 years, and has been enshrined in temples and revered through festivals, poetry and art. He is more of a psychological reality, indifferent to rationality and evidence. The first is historical (a person), the second mythological (an idea). For rationalists, both Krishnas are false. For nationalists, only the historical Krishna is real.

The rationalists align with eighteenth-century 'modern'

notions of what constitutes truth: it needs to be material and measurable. This informs the scientific rules of historiography, following which no honest historian can prove the existence of a historical Krishna; or, for that matter, the historic Abraham of Judaism, Christianity and Islam; or Achilles and Odysseus of the Greeks. This upsets nationalists, who react violently when their leaps of faith are deemed unscientific.

Ironically, both rationalists and nationalists do not value psychological reality, or 'meaning', which forms the cornerstone of Vedic thought. Truth in the Vedas is not a thing, but a thought about that thing. What distinguishes humans from all other living creatures is that we give meaning to the things we shape our lives on. The value of Jesus, Muhammad, the Buddha and Krishna comes not from their physical existence but from the meaning they bring to people's lives. In other words, the idea of Krishna, more than the physical existence, is what has shaped India over the centuries.

The story of Krishna, like the story of Rama, along with stories of Vishnu and Shiva, started being codified and written down in the post-Buddhist period to challenge monastic ideals. Thus, the earliest Mahabharata, which tells the story of Krishna's adulthood, has been dated to 300 BCE and 300 CE, between the collapse of the Mauryan Empire and the rise of the Gupta Empire, in the period that saw the rise of Indo-Greek and Kushana kings. This epic also contains the Bhagavad Gita, where Krishna explains the essence of Vedic philosophy to the archer-prince Arjuna. The story of

Krishna's childhood comes to us from the Gupta period, approximately 400 CE, in the Harivamsa that vividly describes his cowherd roots, and by 1000 CE, we have the Bhagavata Purana elaborating his famous dance with the milkmaids, the rasaleela. Radha, from whom Krishna is inseparable today, appeared in her full glory only in the twelfth-century *Geeta Govinda* by the poet Jayadeva, though we find a proto-Radha called Pinnai in Tamil Sangam literature dated to 500 CE. In all likelihood, the idea of Krishna emerges only in the period after the Mauryan Empire, marking the break from old Vedic ritual-based Hinduism, and the rise of Puranic story-based and temple-based Hinduism.

Krishna, like Rama, presents the idea that material life matters as much as spiritual life, hence both the Mahabharata and the Ramayana are essentially property disputes, the throne of Hastinapur in one and the throne of Ayodhya in the other. They introduce and elaborate the idea of dharma—where we function focusing not just on the 'self' (sva-dharma, jiva-atma) but also the 'other' (para-dharma, param-atma). Rama follows rules perfectly (maryada-purushottam) while Krishna bends rules (leela-purushottam) to uphold dharma. Yet, it is Krishna alone who is considered divinity in totality (purna-avatar), greater than even Rama for, unlike Rama, he also embraces aesthetic, romantic and even erotic emotions.

This sensual side of Hinduism was shunned by the rise of the Vedanta monastic order, a thousand years ago, led by Adi Shankara and later Ramanuja and Madhava. They reframed Buddhist monastic ideals, but gave preference to the hermit over the householder. And so, beyond the Gangetic plains most Krishna temples, be it Pandharpur in Maharashtra, Udupi in Karnataka or Guruvayoor in Kerala, prefer to see Krishna alone, without Radha. The trend is to see Krishna as the child, the warrior, the teacher, but not the lover.

The rejection of the sensual and the feminine amplified itself in Victorian times, as colonial powers saw Indians as 'effeminate'. Determined to prove the colonial powers wrong, Indian freedom fighters embraced celibacy as a sign of love for Mother India. The result of this can be seen in the Jagannatha Temple, Puri, Odisha, where Krishna is enshrined with his siblings. This temple, over 800 years old, includes a bhoga-mandapa (pleasure pavilion), a natya-mandapa (theatre pavilion) and an ananda-bazaar (market of bliss), indicating a joyful exploration of the sensory. However, over time, the culture of the maharis (devadasis), women who sang and danced to the Gita Govinda for centuries, has been wiped out, as they were deemed prostitutes. Now only men control the shrine: pandas (priests) renowned for their corruption, and now monks of the Puri mathas who are seeking to increase their authority.

When the Muslims entered India, Krishna started being worshipped secretly in havelis, or households of Rajasthan and Gujarat, and not in grand temples. This was a practice started by Vallabha Acharya so that Rajputs could protect the legacy of Krishna from marauders. But over the centuries many Muslim poet-saints, like Salabega of seventeenth-century Odisha or Hasrat Mohani of the twentieth century, composed songs in praise of Krishna. This paradox captures the spirit of India, but the right-wing focuses only on the former, and the left-wing on the latter. Neither is comfortable with the purna-purusha (complete man) sporting a woman's plait for his hairstyle, seen in sculptures of Odisha and the iconography of Srinathji in Nathdvara, thus revealing his comfort with gender fluidity. In seeking our own political agenda, many of us lose sight of the modernity embedded in the idea of Krishna, where happiness exists in embracing worldly life with its myriad sensual and spiritual complexities, rather than seeking to reject or control it.

45

Epics as novels

Most people in India are not familiar with the Sanskrit Ramayana or Mahabharata. We read popular versions, which in turn are based on regional retellings, which began appearing less than 1,000 years ago and became very prevalent from around 500 years ago.

Many regional works are either lost, as they were orally transmitted, or exist in fragments, awaiting translations. As a result, not many people in Gujarat, for example, are familiar with the poetic works of Bhalan (fifteenth century) and Premananda (seventeenth century) known as akhyanas, based on epic episodes. Outside literary circles, few are aware of the existence of the Gujarati *Giridhar Ramayana*.

Regional retellings are not translations or exact reproductions, but rather innovative retellings. They are broadly faithful to the Sanskrit work, but they do have many deviations. For example, the Bengali Ramayana by Krittibasa has the first reference to the Lakshmana-rekha and to the dhobi gossiping about Sita's reputation. In the Kannada Ramayana we find the tale of Ravana unable to lift the Shiva bow, and so unable to marry Sita, while in the Malayalam Ramayana we find the tale of Ravana probably being Sita's father.

Sarala Das in his Odiya Mahabharata tells the backstory of Shakuni, how his family was killed by Duryodhana, which makes Shakuni not the epic villain but the epic victim, who hated the Kauravas. Many of these works even shift the geography of the tale: so Balaram Das makes Rama visit Puri in Odisha, while Villiputturar makes Arjuna visit Srirangam in Tamil Nadu.

Most regional retellings seek to establish the divinity of Rama and Krishna, for they were composed in the time when bhakti, or passionate devotion, became the dominant expression of Hinduism. So, it is not surprising that preference is given either to the upright Rama or the loveable child Krishna of the Bhagavata than to the more complex adult Krishna of the Mahabharata. These works are conscious of being holy books, retellings of exploits of venerable characters. They did not see themselves as secular entertainment.

However, from the eighteenth century, the novel as a literary form became popular in Europe and it fired the imagination of Indian authors after being introduced to India in the nineteenth century. Indians began writing novels based on the Ramayana and the Mahabharata.

Here, they were not self-consciously holy. They told a story either as the all-seeing storyteller or through the eyes of a character, often playing the role of a lawyer or judge, defending the case of one character while prosecuting others. There is a strong urge to connect the ancient tale to everyday modern experience. This has led to the rise of the genre known as mythological fiction, popular in regional languages and in English, some in prose, some in poetry. These often endorse modern political ideologies, as a result of which many readers of these modern novels assume they communicate 'Vedic' truth.

It is significant that in the bhakti period people preferred the Ramayana over the Mahabharata, and there was great desire to show Rama and Krishna as embodiments of perfection. In novel-writing modern times, there is a greater preference for the Mahabharata over the Ramayana, and the desire to find faults in Rama and Krishna, more flawed humans and less perfect gods.

46

The girl who chose

About a thousand years ago, a remarkable thing happened in India. We find a rapid rise of regional languages and scripts, giving rise to the modern languages of India. And the first and most popular piece of literature to be composed, and recomposed, by several poets in most of these languages happens to be the epic Ramayana. Here, the nayaka (ideal protagonist) of earlier Sanskrit plays, the avatar (abbreviated form of the infinite divine) of the Sanskrit Puranas, becomes Bhagavan, or God. Every one of these poets claims to be inspired by the Valmiki Ramayana, composed over 2,000 years ago, but each one gives the story a twist of their own. What is consistent is the regal nature of Rama, his nobility and augustness. He is, after all, the only form of God in Hinduism to be visualized as king. When Western academicians started studying the Ramayana, they did so, naturally, with Western prejudices, which included on the one hand the notion of a Christian god who died for the sins of man and on the other, the doctrine of equality and social justice. Viewed through this template, all Hindu gods appear inadequate, especially Rama, the God-king.

This template is only now being called out. But the damage is done. Writers on the Ramayana are obliged to play a courtroom game, where Rama is being constantly prosecuted for being problematic. The defenders are deemed 'right radicals' and the prosecutors are imagined as 'left liberals'.

But, as we have heard so many times on the streets of Mumbai: *nazar badlee to nazara badla*—when the gaze changes, the world changes. Time to break free from this right–left game of those who love to dominate. Then a new Ramayana emerges, or rather the older one, one of Valmiki Ramayana. It explains why Rama was admired—albeit for different reasons—by Hindus, Jains and Buddhists as well as the people of South-east Asia, in Camodia and Thailand and Bali and Myanmar.

Suddenly you realize the many conflicts of the narrative: How to be decent in an unfair world? How to love a man who will follow the family rules, even if the rules are unfair? How to love a woman who has her own mind? How never to deny dignity to the man who does not respect any rules or choices? How to accept suffering that follows when you punish someone? How to accept misfortune that is not of your own making? How to raise children with love, not hatred for the father who abandoned them? How to let go without taking away the dignity of those who are rejected?

Hinduism has no concept of Judgement Day. God is no judge in Hinduism. Yet, we find Hindu 'leaders' passing judgement all the time. Why? Wherefrom came this template, or this desire to turn humans into hero, villain or victim? From Christian mythology? From Greek mythology?

Time to seek alternative templates. Discover the world where no one is good or bad. Where there are only rules, choices, consequences and no guarantees. How do we then live our life with responsibility and without blame? This is the divine world of the Ramayana, where a girl who could choose fell in love with a prince who was bound to follow rules.

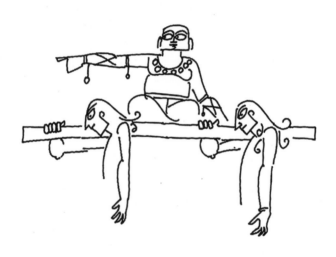

47

Travelling from thought to thought

 In the Rig Veda, dated conservatively to 1500 BCE, a poet-sage wonders, 'What came first? What existed before the first?' Thus, he travels, not physically but mentally, and explores new worlds. Ramana Maharshi, a twentieth-century mystic, reflects this sentiment when he said that from his abode in Arunachalam he travelled the world. Travel then is not just physical, from one place to another, but also mental, from one thought to another. The outer journey made sense only when it was accompanied by an inner journey, at least to the rishis, the poet-sages of India, whose hymns make up the venerated Vedas. They were the seers: those who saw what no one else saw.

We do know that the rishis travelled a lot: they travelled east from the banks of the River Saraswati to the banks of the River Ganga in the west, when the former dried up;

their songs celebrating that once-grand river are found in the Vedas. They travelled south from the Gangetic plains to the river valleys of the Godavari and the Kaveri, as we learn from the stories of Agastya and Rama in the epic Ramayana. They were the first explorers. But they did not travel to conquer; they sought to understand the human condition. In the epic Mahabharata, when the Pandavas are exiled, they are told to follow the path of the rishis, visit holy places, talk to sages and strangers, so as to expand the mind.

Expanding the mind is a constant theme of the Vedas. The hymns constantly evoke the brahman, meaning 'the great' or 'the expanded one'. Eventually, the word came to mean God. The term 'brahman' comes from the Sanskrit roots 'brh', meaning to expand, and 'manas', meaning the mind. Brahman then is one of infinitely expanded mind. The brahmin (before it became infamous) referred to that which enables expansion of the mind. It referred to the scriptures that explained mind-expanding rituals, as well as the men who memorized the scripture and the details of the ritual.

The ritual called the yagna was a journey that enabled the performer to travel to the realm of the gods, the realm of ideas, and experience ecstasy and immortality that was in short supply in the mundane world. It was perhaps what we now call an adrenaline rush! That is why the hymns simultaneously refer to the stars and the rivers and the forests, as well as to the mind and the senses and the heart. The divide between the physical and mental is so subtle that interpreters are not sure if the Vedic hymns refer to the mundane world or to the metaphysical world. Perhaps they refer to both: as one travelled from place to place, one also travelled from thought to thought. Destination of the long journey over highways, rituals, trade routes and pilgrim trails, then, was also enlightenment.

48

Money maya

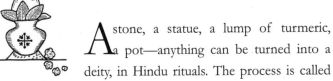 A stone, a statue, a lump of turmeric, a pot—anything can be turned into a deity, in Hindu rituals. The process is called prana-pratishtha. Ritually, an object is made divine for a finite period of time. After that period, the divinity leaves the venerated object, and the object—like a corpse—is consigned to water. Thus, the ritual mimics the cycle of life and death. So it is with currency notes. One day, a piece of paper has value. Rupees 500. Rupees 1,000. The next day it does not. Only here, the avahan (invocation) and the visarjan (farewell) is done by the state, embodied in the prime minister and implemented through the Reserve Bank of India.

This unique ability of humans to infuse value and meaning into anything is called maya. According to Yuval Harare, author of *Sapiens,* it is the collective fiction that sustains humanity. It helps us collaborate and establish societies. As a historian who is an outsider, he has the luxury of calling it 'fiction'—but it is 'fact' for the insider. It is perhaps more respectful to call these narratives myths subjective truths, real for believers, unreal for non-believers.

Maya is not illusion (something that does not exist). It is delusion (a deliberate misunderstanding of what does exist). Printed paper does exist. It's a fact. That it is money is a belief, like justice, like equality, like God. The state functions like a priest, establishing God and justice and equality through ritual and argument. Once we buy into the narrative God, justice, equality and money become real.

Without myths, there can be no culture. Myths, hence cultures, are a function of place, time and people. For example, 2,500 years ago, in Babylon, no one would have understood words like Allah or Jesus, but they would have understood Marduk, the supreme God, the most powerful god of that time. Likewise, the Indian rupee note, issued by the Indian state, would have made no sense to the Buddha, or to Chandragupta or Chanakya.

Indian philosophy distinguishes between truths dependent on a context (maya) and truths independent of context (satya). The human ability to create value is eternal, hence satya. But what humans value—be it money, or state, or politicians, or ideology, or deity—is temporary, hence maya. Food is satya. Money is maya. Starvation is satya. But poverty? That's a tough one. For the sage who is naked, who has no possessions, is technically a 'have-not', but he does not consider himself poor.

The most primitive tribe in the world will understand

human craving for food. But not everyone will understand the modern obsession for bundles of printed paper, or digits in a database appearing on a screen that has the power to make a person rich or poor, powerful or powerless.

People make fun of people who worship stones because here both parties have not bought into the myth. But no one makes fun of people who stash paper in their homes, or smile gleefully on seeing numbers received on a smartphone app, because everyone has bought into the myth of money. Such is the power of myth. Recognition of this has led sages to popularize that ubiquitous Indian phrase, '*Sab maya hai!*'

49

Single fathers

One day, while wandering through the countryside, Matsyendranath saw a farmer's wife crying in front of her house. He divined that she was childless. He gave her a fistful of ash and said, 'Consume it and you will become pregnant.' The lady accepted the ash but a few hours later was consumed by doubt and fear. She threw the ash in a pit where her family threw cow dung to make manure. Twelve years later, Matsyendranath passed by the same house and, on seeing the woman, said, 'Where is your son? He must be around eleven now!' The lady did not know what to say but the look on her face revealed all. 'You did not consume that ash, did you? You did not trust my powers. Tell me where you threw the ash.' The lady took the sage to the cow dung manure pit. Matsyendranath dug through the manure and pulled out a beautiful eleven-year-old boy. 'The ash I gave you was so powerful that it transformed into a child even outside your womb, in your cow dung manure pit. This son would have been your son. But now I claim him as my son. Born in a cow dung pit, I name him Gorakshanath.' The farmer's wife, still childless, begged for forgiveness. The sage simply smiled and walked away with his son. He had chosen the life of a hermit, yet clearly, his masters wanted him to be a father. Gorakshanath went on to become a great Nath-jogi like his father. Some would say, even more powerful.

How does one read this story? Is it the story of a single dad, a man who becomes a father even though he has no wife? Such tales of men who become fathers without wives is a recurring theme in Hindu mythology.

Drona, the great tutor of the Kauravas and the Pandavas, had no mother. His father, Bharadvaja, saw an apsara and was so aroused that he ejaculated on the spot and the semen fell in a pot. Here, it transformed into a child, a boy, who was named Drona, the pot-born, raised by his father, but not a mother.

His wife Kripi and her twin Kripa were born when another sage called Sharadwan saw a nymph called Janapadi and ejaculated on river reeds. Like Drona, they had a father, but no mother. But their father did not know of their birth. King Shantanu of Hastinapur found them and raised them. He was single then; his first wife, Ganga, had left him, taking their son, Devavrata, with him, and he was yet to meet his second wife, Satyavati. In other words, Kripa and Kripi were adopted by a single father.

The famous beauty, Shakuntala, was conceived when her

mother, an apsara, enchanted and seduced the great sage Vishwamitra. But she abandoned the child on the forest floor. Vishwamitra refused to accept the child. So the child remained on the forest floor, attracting the attention of vultures. A sage called Kanva came upon this abandoned child and adopted her as his own. Thus, Kanva was a single father of an adopted child.

All these tales open our minds about alternative forms of families, where fathers can have children without a wife, and children of single fathers grow up to be healthy adults.

50

Accommodating the queer

Once upon a time, there was a monk in a Buddhist monastery who approached other monks to 'defile' (dusatha, in Pali) him. He probably meant sex, for in Buddhist lore, sexual desire was seen as contaminating one away from the path of dhamma. The monks refused and so he approached the mahouts or elephant-keepers who lived in the vicinity of the monastery. The mahouts obliged, but after the act, started grumbling and speaking ill about the monastery and its residents. The monk was identified as a pandaka and it was decreed that a pandaka should not be ordained as a monk, owing to his inability to restrain his sexual urges. In fact, some went to the extent of saying that the pandaka can never attain enlightenment.

This story comes from the *Vinaya Pitaka,* one of the earliest books of the Buddhist canon, listing rules for monks and monasteries and attributed to the Buddha himself. But it has undergone much revision due to oral transmission and several editors.

Who was the pandaka? Answers are varied: from eunuch, homosexual, passive effeminate homosexual, transgendered male, to an intersex or even sexless being. Further, Buddhist commentators such as Buddhaghosha, Asanga and Yashomitra refer to various types of pandakas: the pandaka-by-fortnight (pakka-pandaka); the pandaka-by-castration (opakkamika-pandaka); the pandaka-who-performs-oral-sex (asittaka-pandaka); the impotent-pandaka (napunsaka-pandaka); the voyeur-pandaka (ussuya-pandaka).

Further, the Buddhist canon does not presume a world of two genders: male and female. There is reference to many kinds of transgender persons located in the spectrum of gender: the man-like woman (vepurisika), the sexually ambiguous (sambhinna), the androgyne (ubhatovyanjanaka). This reveals, at the very least, an awareness of queer people, certainly transgender persons, and probably effeminate gays and masculine lesbians.

Buddhism had no problem with their existence, but assumes that their libido and lack of sexual restraint is greater than that of heterosexual men (as many still do today). Similar discomfort is revealed in matters related to women, who were seen by ancient Buddhist writers as having greater sexual urges than men (quite unlike what most people believe today). Eventually women were ordained, but were lower down in the hierarchy and segregated from men. The queers were firmly kept out.

In Thailand today, the word pandaka is translated as 'kathoey' and is used for cross-dressing homosexuals and transgenders, who are very much part of mainstream society, though again not quite welcome within the monastic order. This word is closely related to the word 'kothi', used by cross-dressing homosexuals and transgenders of India to identify themselves. Perhaps the word either spread from India to Thailand or from Thailand to India 1,000 years ago, when there was a thriving sea trade between India and South-east Asia.

In ancient India, sex was not bad. It was a pleasurable activity (kama) that often distracted people from doing their social duties (dharma), that could be a source of income (artha) for courtesans, and a distraction for monks who sought liberation (moksha). Sex was not just an act between man and woman. There is an open acceptance of the third gender, indicated by the presence of a wide variety of words in Sanskrit and Prakrit and regional literature that speaks of men who are not quite men and women who are not quite women, and a whole diverse range of beings. Sex with these beings cannot be hetero-normative. So along with diverse gender, there is acknowledgement of diverse sexualities.

In Sanskrit literature, there are references to tales of women turning into men—the most famous is Shikhandi in the Mahabharata. Bhishma refuses to see him as a man and Krishna insists that he is a man, though he was born with a woman's body, and only after marriage, thanks to the intervention of a yaksha, managed to acquire male genitalia.

Then there is Yuvanashva, the king who drinks the magic potion meant for his wives and gets pregnant, and bears a child called Mandhata, whom he cannot nurse as he has no breasts and so no milk to offer. Indra comes down to earth and cuts his thumb and lets the infant Mandhata drink his blood (the blood of gods is made of milk, we are told). Thus Mandhata's mother and wet nurse are both men. It is not uncommon in art to see the goddess represented as a peacock (as in the Kapaleshwara temple in Chennai), not peahen. And to see motifs showing two peacocks dancing like lovers, both joyfully displaying their plumage.

Both Buddhism and Hinduism fought to gain mind space in the Indic mind. Buddhism was uncomfortable with transgender persons in monasteries but had no issues with them in mainstream society. Hinduism had issues with them in mainstream society but accommodated them in temples, which is why there are many traditions in India where transgenders are closely linked to deities: so there are the Kinnaras and Mangal-mukhis of north India who worship Bahucharji, the Jogatas of Belgaum region who worship Yellamma, and the Aravanis of Tamil Nadu who see themselves as bride-widows of Aravan, a form of Shiva, who was Arjuna's son by a Naga princess. They are part of local fertility rites. In the recently concluded Kumbh Mela of Ujjain, the Simhastha—a Kinnara akhada—was established, a transgender mahamandaleshwara was chosen and hundreds of people thronged to get barkat (blessing) from them.

With the arrival of Islam, Buddhism waned from mainstream Indian society while Hindu society became more puritanical, with the rise of Hindu monastic orders (akhada) who saw themselves as defenders of Hinduism. Increasingly, all things sexual were seen as a perversion or the vulgar indulgence of the rich. The culture of employing castrated men, popular in Persia, Central Asia and China, was adopted in India. This gave rise to the hijra community, who were invited to weddings and childbirth festivities to ward off the evil eye, and employed in harems, not yet 'criminal tribes'. In fact, most hijras in India today are expected to embrace Islam and have Muslim names, though worship of Hindu and Christian gods and saints is permitted. The status of these hijras declined with the arrival of the British.

Clearly, Indic culture (a mix of Buddhist, Jain, Hindu and Islamic ways of being) saw transpersons as part of nature's diversity. Were they tolerated in society? We must be careful of such a question, for the books we refer to, the Dharmasutras and the Dharmashastras of the pre-Islamic era, are not canonical, like the Bible or the Quran. They tend to be misogynist and casteist—hardly benchmarks for a modern civil society. We cannot expect them to be highly accommodative of queer genders and sexualities, as their primary aim is to reaffirm and reinforce the merits of a rigid hierarchical society. Further, traditional Indian scriptures continually say that laws are fluid and must change keeping in mind three things: desha (place), kala (time), patra (people). What matters is dharma—which Chanakya acknowledges is that which prevents matsya nyaya (jungle law) from taking over society. With this in mind, all of us have a choice, no matter what the courts decide: accommodate in our hearts the diversity of genders in nature, or suppress them based on views of a few celibate monks and puritans who, either out of monastic discipline, or envy, or fear of pollution, oppose all kind of sexual expression.